I0635927

Praise for *Disability Friendly*

"In *Disability Friendly*, John Kemp offers a personal, direct, and practical masterclass for anyone looking to make the call for equity and inclusion real for people with disabilities. This exceptional book provides a distinct roadmap for all of us to take action in our own lives and workplaces to redress the intractable problems of exclusion, unemployment, stereotypes, and discrimination that have befallen people with disabilities in recent times and throughout the ages."

—**Peter W. Thomas, JD, Managing Partner,**
The Powers Law Firm

"Every CEO who has issued a public statement around their company's commitment to Diversity, Equity and Inclusion needs to read this book. There is no one more credible to take a stand on the subject, and yet Kemp uses openness and curiosity instead of recrimination and rebuke. *Disability Friendly* is a wonderful tool for leaders today and in the future; I expect it to become required reading as more and more organizations recognize that the time for action is now."

—**Charlotte Dales, Founder & CEO, Inclusively.com**

"As Secretary of Labor, I witnessed the power of employment to not only sustain Americans financially, but to enable them to pursue their ambitions and strengthen their sense of dignity and purpose. Unfortunately, people living with disabilities are still held back from fulfilling careers despite employers having more options than ever to make their workplaces fully open and accessible. Thankfully, John Kemp, one of the most passionate and prolific champions in the disability movement, has written this illuminating and entertaining guide to empowering people with disabilities. John directly addresses the misconceptions and excuses that still keep employers from taking practical steps toward supporting disabled employees. He also reminds us of the extraordinary achievements that are possible when we give every person the opportunity to succeed. *Disability Friendly* should inspire our nation to enable every American to reach their highest potential."

—**Elizabeth Dole, President, American Red Cross; US Senator; Founder and Chair, Elizabeth Dole Foundation**

"For any leader who wants to better the workplace to include people with disabilities in their DEI initiative, this is a must-read book. John artfully combines his personal experience with professional knowledge and translates them into actionable recommendations. It is more than learning the best inclusion practices, but about understanding and relating to another human being authentically. Very powerful."

—**Frances West, Founder, FrancesWest&Co**

"*Disability Friendly* should be required reading by anyone who thinks they are serious about equality. The publication comes at a critically important time, as advocates pointing to the Disability Equality Crisis must now struggle even harder to have their voices heard, in a world that still thinks treating you unfairly because you have a disability is completely different (aka not so serious) as treating you unfairly because of any number of other, dare one say competing, identities."

—**Susan Scott-Parker, Founder of Business Disability International; Founder, Disability and Ethical Artificial Intelligence (AI) Alliance**

"Drawing on his deep experience and unique insights, John gives organizations the blueprint they need to engage business leaders, equip them with the knowledge they need and deliver success. It's the why, what, who and how to transform organizations and generate valuable business, social and community benefits. Thank you, John, for this wonderful guide that will help businesses to get it right—because when they do, everybody will win."

—**Suzanne Colbert, AM, Founding CEO (former),**
Australian Network on Disability

"John Kemp's new book, *Disability Friendly: How to Move from Clueless to Inclusive*, lays out a strong rationale for disability inclusion and provides its readers with a Blueprint for accomplishing it! When John Kemp visited Japan as my guest, he delivered this strong message of disability inclusion to Japanese business leaders who embraced his approach well. I strongly urge you to buy this book and use it in every business and organization in every country of the world, as John Kemp lays out an inclusive approach that will work everywhere!"

—**Hiro Itoh, Founder and President,**
Japan Abilities Care-Net, Inc.

"Diversity, equity and inclusion is an important trend in society today. John adds disability inclusion to the mix, so we can all benefit from the skills, talents, and commitment of disabled people in our places of work and play. Disability inclusion truly benefits everyone."

"I'd love to have John spend time with my grandkids who have disabilities. His message is one of hope, courage and legitimacy. And those are the themes of this must-read book."

—**Bill Novelli, Founder, Porter Novelli Agency**

"John Kemp is like a fine wine. He has aged with growing knowledge and continues to be driven to make significant changes that are benefiting our society and others around the world. John is a dynamic speaker who draws people in thus enabling to learn both about the barriers disabled people are facing and the reasons why breaking down barriers in the workplace and society overall makes us all stronger. This book will enable you to learn from John's experiences as well as encourage you to think about what you have done in the past to advance or impede the inclusion of disabled people."

—Judith E. Heumann, International Disability Rights Advocate; author of *Being Heumann* and *Rolling Warrior*

DISABILITY FRIENDLY

Kemp, John D.,
Disability friendly : how to
move from clueless to inclusiv
[2023]
33305253862944
ca   04/06/23

John D. Kemp

DISABILITY FRIENDLY

HOW TO MOVE FROM
CLUELESS

to

WILEY

Copyright © 2023 by John D. Kemp. All rights reserved.

Published by John Wiley & Sons, Inc., Hoboken, New Jersey.
Published simultaneously in Canada.

No part of this publication may be reproduced, stored in a retrieval system, or transmitted in any form or by any means, electronic, mechanical, photocopying, recording, scanning, or otherwise, except as permitted under Section 107 or 108 of the 1976 United States Copyright Act, without either the prior written permission of the Publisher, or authorization through payment of the appropriate per-copy fee to the Copyright Clearance Center, Inc., 222 Rosewood Drive, Danvers, MA 01923, (978) 750-8400, fax (978) 750-4470, or on the web at www.copyright.com. Requests to the Publisher for permission should be addressed to the Permissions Department, John Wiley & Sons, Inc., 111 River Street, Hoboken, NJ 07030, (201) 748-6011, fax (201) 748-6008, or online at http://www.wiley.com/go/permission.

Limit of Liability/Disclaimer of Warranty: While the publisher and author have used their best efforts in preparing this book, they make no representations or warranties with respect to the accuracy or completeness of the contents of this book and specifically disclaim any implied warranties of merchantability or fitness for a particular purpose. No warranty may be created or extended by sales representatives or written sales materials. The advice and strategies contained herein may not be suitable for your situation. You should consult with a professional where appropriate. Further, readers should be aware that websites listed in this work may have changed or disappeared between when this work was written and when it is read. Neither the publisher nor authors shall be liable for any loss of profit or any other commercial damages, including but not limited to special, incidental, consequential, or other damages.

For general information on our other products and services or for technical support, please contact our Customer Care Department within the United States at (800) 762-2974, outside the United States at (317) 572-3993 or fax (317) 572-4002.

Wiley also publishes its books in a variety of electronic formats. Some content that appears in print may not be available in electronic formats. For more information about Wiley products, visit our web site at www.wiley.com.

Library of Congress Cataloging-in-Publication Data is Available:

ISBN 9781119830092 (Cloth)
ISBN 9781119830214 (ePub)
ISBN 9781119830221 (ePDF)

Cover Design and Image: Wiley

SKY10035809_082322

I dedicate this book to my wife, Sameta ("Sam"), with whom I share an extraordinary life of love, laughter, family, friends, and fulfillment in every way.

Contents

Foreword

People with disabilities make up an estimated 1 billion, or 15%, of the world's population. About 80% are of working age. The right of people with disabilities to fully participate in society, live as full citizens, as productive employees is often hampered by discriminatory practices and negative stigmas. There's not one aspect of life where people with disabilities should not expect to participate in every way.

From my global vantage point, I know this "exclusion" remains the costly mistake of today. Representation on all levels remains scarce but we are at a global tipping point in which our stark absence within positions of leadership is no longer being overlooked. I am an award-winning social entrepreneur, dangerous dreamer, and founder of the Valuable 500—a global business collective made up of 500 CEOs and their companies, innovating together for Disability Inclusion.

Over the past two decades, I have set up several organizations and initiatives centered on disability business inclusion. I was recently appointed president of the IAPB, and I sit on several diversity and inclusion boards including L'Oréal and Sky. John Kemp and I have been friends and colleagues for more than 20 years, and this book provides a wonderful insight into how institutions can embed Disability Inclusion practices into their fabric to ensure that people can unapologetically show up to their place of work, education, or retail outlets as their whole selves without fears of it being inaccessible.

It is nonsensical that some employers are willing to forego recruiting disabled talent by maintaining inaccessible build environments or inaccessible websites. There is a vast untapped pool of disabled talent looking to work and many people with disabilities are reliable and skilled individuals with the potential to belong fully to the world of work in all industries and types of positions. Moreover, it is also nonsensical that retailers would intentionally jeopardize the profits that could be made from sales to people with disabilities as well as their friends and families. It is no longer "acceptable" for companies to not address the impact of their "exclusionary" policies. The savviest companies understand the high cost of exclusion and are aware that Disability Inclusion positively affects their bottom lines.

Disability Friendly is high-level learning about Disability Culture and how it translates into empowered people with disabilities who merely want to live lives of opportunities. For businesses engaged with the Valuable 500, they understand that people with disabilities must be an essential part of their workforces, their customer bases, their supply chains, and people with disabilities expect to be included as well. Undeniably "inclusion for all" is not a linear path, but the first step is to acknowledge that balancing individual and collective needs requires us to share. We need to eradicate the psychology of scarcity and the notion that "if I give to you, I take away from myself." It has been proven time and time again that diversity has significant organizational benefits. You do not get to pick and mix inclusion—it is either in its entirety or not at all. Inclusion is about choice, equitable investment of resources, and leadership.

For Diversity, Equity, and Inclusion executives, this book explains why issues of disability, and people with disabilities, are an absolutely necessary component to advancing their employers' goals. To leave people with disabilities out of DEI initiatives is highly negligent as disability affects all of us. In fact, 83% of disabilities are acquired, whether due to an accident, illness, or genetic condition. Organizations that include Disability Inclusion in their D&I agenda are better prepared to support employees through life's events. That's because they have initiatives and tools in place to help employees adjust to new ways of working and living. Empathy, tenacity, and resilience are just a few of the characteristics associated with disabled people. By including disability in the D&I agenda, businesses are better placed to attract and retain such talent.

At 28, I finally came out of the disability closet. It was my leap into the world. I could no longer hide my limited eyesight and quite frankly I was exhausted. I vowed to be proud of my capabilities, that I would never apologize for having a disability, and I would fight for every disabled person's right to be included fairly and equitably. I want everybody's true nature to be able to shine. While my advocacy journey has not been easy—I've had several doors shut in my face and a multitude of barriers to break—it has never caused me to veer away from pursuing equity, economic independence, full societal participation for well over one billion people with disabilities like John and me. We will never stop using our inherent powers and we will never stop speaking up and out about wrongs that can so easily be righted.

As a society, we need to stop putting so much emphasis on labels because labels are for jam jars. We are extraordinary, different, wonderful people who are not defined by the box we tick. Currently, disability is often considered as something more akin to being weak or dependent but there is a wealth of talent that is not being utilized for their insight, innovation, and potential. By moving past the medical model of disability and recognizing the societal structures that serve as a barrier for many we can truly begin to balance the playing field.

Enjoy delving into *Disability Friendly*. John has interwoven key gems wrapped in his humor, and I am certain you will learn a great deal from the following chapters!

Caroline Casey
Founder
The Valuable 500

Acknowledgments

To the many corporate leaders and disability leaders and influencers who have guided me and even hired me, I still learned more than I was able to share with you, and I synthesized from all of you the wisdom you shared with ease and confidence, I thank you! Frances West, Felicity Spowart and PJ Edington (deceased); Delta's Ed Bastian, John Laughter, Dana Folsom, Alison Lathrop and Donise Hall; Michael, Carole, Amy Marks Dornbusch, and Justin Marks; Iris and Saul Katz; Ralph and Lucy Palleschi; and Michael and Chris Pascucci, Sheryl Buchel, Mike Caprara, Dr. Chris Rosa, Victor Calise, Russ Cusick, Candy Cucharo, and Beth Daly.

To my law partners at The Powers Firm, Peter "Lloyd" Thomas, managing partner, and Bobby Silverstein, partner and lead author of the Americans with Disabilities Act; thank you!

To my global family of extraordinary disability advocates and leaders: Paul Hearne (deceased), Kathy Martinez, Jim Weisman, Patricia (Pat) Wright, Judy Heumann, Andy Imparato, Caroline Casey, Susan Scott-Parker, Jill Houghton, Deb Dagit, Jennifer Sheehy, Lori Golden, Charlotte Dales, Sarah Bernard and Charles Trunz of Inclusively, Justin (deceased) and Yoshiko Dart, Michael Morris, Susan Constantino, Ed Mathews, Duncan Wyeth, Amena El-Saie and Ramez Maher (Egypt), Axel Leblois, Jenny Lay-Flurrie, Hiro Itoh (Japan), Susan Scott-Parker, US Senator Tom Harkin, Suzanne Colbert and Dr. Dinesh Palipana (Australia), Maria Town, Claudia Gordon, Jonathan

Young, Dr. Glen White, Justin Constantine (deceased); Col. Greg Gadson, Dr. Satendra Singh, Jim Gibbons, Susan Daniels (deceased), Deb McFadden, Mark Johnson, Mark Wafer, Dr. Rory Cooper, Neil Jacobson, Marlee Matlin, Susan Sygall, Lex Frieden, Rosangela Berman Bieler, Cong. Jim Langevin, Michael Stein, Carol Glazer, Gordon Skinner, John Garrison, Meg O'Connell, and so many others, thank you!

To my dear and most distinguished friend of 53 years, Senator Bob Dole, who passed away while I was writing this book. Your wisdom and wit, your brilliance in policy and strategy, and your political acumen nearly lifted you to the US presidency, thank you for our sincere friendship. And to his magnificent wife, Senator Elizabeth Dole, for our friendship and the honor of serving on your foundation's board, thank you!

To my colleagues at Wiley—Richard Narramore, Julie Kerr, Jessica Filippo—and drafters/researchers Matt Conlin and Jenna Lamm, who worked endless hours to assist me in finalizing this book, and to my Lakeshore Foundation colleague Brittany Elkins and Lakeshore Foundation Board Chair Greg Johnston, our Board members, and executive staff, for your strong support that allowed me to complete this book, thank you!

Finally, I owe unlimited gratitude to my wife, Sameta (Sam), who has guided and supported me to conceptualize and complete the writing of *Disability Friendly*, and through a career in law and national nonprofit organizations' leadership. Sam committed her life, long before we first met, to empowering people with disabilities and chronic health conditions, every day and in every way. There's no finer, better, smarter, more beautiful, or stronger person with the highest character and greatest personal integrity than Sam. These words will have to suffice for the tremendous respect I hold for you and how you have contributed so completely to the quality of my life, and our lives together. I thank you for this book, and for the wonderful, incredible life we enjoy together.

For all that my dad, my sisters, Kathy Lehmann and Mary Harding, have meant to Sam and me, along with their spouses and families, I express my sincerest thanks and, I promise, I didn't include anything that could embarrass you, though I did try! Thank you to my dear friend Steve Nauheim, and the very best advocate and "Lloyd" who's ever lived, Paul Hearne; another "Lloyd" and friend, John Lancaster.

May our life's work be enhanced by the adoption of these ideas and may people with disabilities flourish in full employment in the months and years ahead.

Introduction

*D*isability Friendly is bold, hip, clever, funny, edgy, and conversational; it differs somewhat from scholarly writings in that it's based in practicality, pragmatism, and proven practices. It requires a new way of thinking about the capabilities of people with disabilities to contribute at all levels of an enterprise, whether in a for-profit organization, an NGO, or the public sector. It requires fundamental changes in the way non-disabled people regard people with all types of disabilities, and how we all work to increase substantially the currently dismal rate of labor force participation by people with disabilities.

There are many in the business community who have not yet fully incorporated disability into their diversity and inclusion strategies and practices and those who want to be better at it. These professionals span the C-suite executives; diversity and inclusion officers; diversity, equity and inclusion officers; senior HR executives; and chief technology and/or information officers. This book will provide the background and context for what has occurred over the last 50 years in moving (inching, really) Disability Inclusion forward, and offer a blueprint for now and the future for all professionals as well as all the dedicated employees and entrepreneurs who want people with disabilities to be included in all aspects of corporate and societal life, where we rightfully belong!

With but a 1–2% increase in the labor force participation rate of people with disabilities since the passage of the

Americans with Disabilities Act in 1990, many new and different approaches must be taken to alter this flat-lined rate. This is not progress; this is maintenance of the status quo at best.

As a person with a disability from birth and who has played an active leadership role in the domestic and international disability movement from the employer perspective, I believe I am as qualified to offer new thoughts and ideas, new processes, and programs, as anyone; not more than, just equal to the most progressive new problem solvers with disabilities.

My life has been an example of an American family facing extraordinary obstacles: a middle child of three siblings born missing most of my arms and legs; our Mother passing away 15 months later from ovarian cancer, and only 3 months after giving birth to my younger sister; our extraordinary father who, at age 32, picked himself up and rebuilt a life of professionalism, faith, profoundly skilled single parenting, and great sacrifices, to afford for each of his three children to flourish in their lives, and for them to "achieve." It was my father's promise to Mother as she was dying that "Johnny" must be given every opportunity to succeed, whether through the acquisition of knowledge, experience, and vision, or his developed personality, and/or pure persistence. My father devoted his life to bettering the lives of others, and we three children benefited from that as well.

Twenty years ago, I married the finest person I've ever met, my wife, Sameta. She was serving as an executive with United Cerebral Palsy's affiliate in Birmingham, Alabama, when we met. We share our deep belief that people with disabilities must be included in all aspects of life, and especially in employment, and if they do so people with disabilities can enjoy the economic freedoms that have eluded too many of us for far too long. Sam is the number one reason I am able to pursue and maintain so many leadership positions, and she has fulfilled my life by providing me with her—and our—wonderful families and five extraordinary grandsons. This aspect of my life, and the lives of so many of us living with disabilities, cannot be understated.

In *Disability Friendly*, I praise publicly several great, effective employer programs, and call out those that should be modified, suspended, or ceased altogether, whether they stem from the federal, state, local, for-profit, or nonprofit levels. We have seen significant societal disruptions to our many traditions in recent years. Some stem from the COVID pandemic; others have been shifting in the years before. What does work mean to so many people with disabilities, some of whom currently work at subminimum-wage positions? What policy and program changes must occur if subminimum wages are no longer allowed? These are important and necessary questions to ask as the movement for Disability Inclusion continues its progress. This book is my attempt to address those questions and put forth some solutions to keep our ribbon of progress moving forward.

Disability can be acquired at any age—from birth on, through any point in life—and people with disabilities can acquire secondary and tertiary disabilities as well; disability can be episodic and even be quieted for periods of time. Disability oftentimes is not visible, which can lead to accusations of "faker" and encourage, unjustifiably at times, "doubters." And it can rise with age, and the ability to perform functions can be more complicated throughout life, and after acquiring a disability. Technology, while beloved by many of us, has yet to be adequately pushed further and higher to assist people living with and emerging into disability to assist in work performance.

People with disabilities are citizens, entitled to all the opportunities that nondisabled people may take for granted—such as using public transportation to get to work, or using productivity enhancements or success enablers to accommodate or overcome any limitations we may have. And we must recognize that the nondisabled can age into disability as they climb the corporate ramp. Why is this important? Every smart employer or public corporation should want to retain and embrace the abilities of older employees to contribute positively to the company's bottom line; their own financial bottom line, their families' social, emotional, and economic well-being; and their communities' economies and strengths. To do otherwise has oppressed extraordinary human beings and their potential to be extremely productive, costing needless dollars to be spent on dependency and caretaking programs for far too many people with disabilities.

The time has come to design work and its processes to embrace contributing citizens of our nation and the world and redeploy those dependency payments to more productive, dignified societal uses.

I also explore in this book how the nature of work is changing dramatically, taking its cues from the COVID pandemic and remote work, as well as personal branding and "entrepreneurship," selling our "goods and services" to consumers and as suppliers of our work product into a final good or service. Some people with disabilities do not work in competitive employment due to transportation and personal assistance limitations. Thus, working as entrepreneurs—as a choice and not as a consequence of workplace discrimination, and delivering work product based on time, cost, quality and quantity standard—helps to overcome these barriers and becomes a great opportunity for people with disabilities. Let's support them!

With the post-pandemic "new normal" now upon us, there are more and easier ways to accommodate all employees and especially applicants and employees with disabilities. What works well for us, like remote working, flexible scheduling, using assistive technologies to perform work, will enable a company's entire workforce to reach higher levels of outputs, throughputs, goal attainment and employee engagement than ever before. There is no better time to take advantage of the disruptions we have all faced in recent years to improve upon and create opportunities for everyone, making Disability Inclusion a core focus of how we reenvision what it means to be inclusive, what it means to work, and what it means to provide employees with the tools to succeed.

Disability Friendly offers you a blueprint to move forward by engaging all corporate and community groups in your enterprise with cross-enterprise guidance. Including people with disabilities in your workforce is a multitiered, complex process that requires the engagement of numerous departments and divisions, and must be led and championed by the chief executive officer and strongly supported by C-suite executives to be fully successful. Our employees expect corporations and all employers to live up to the call for a responsive, compassionate, high-performing organization that is sustainable and allows all employees to thrive. The disability-friendly blueprint should make this effort easier to accomplish.

I just know you will be great and inclusive in the years ahead!

What the World Is Missing When It Overlooks People with Disabilities

In Part I of *Disability Friendly*, I explore the concept of Disability Inclusion and the consequences society faces for not more fully including those of us with disabilities. Besides the unspeakable human toll it takes on a person's self-esteem, self-respect, and ability to contribute to "our more perfect Union," people without disabilities miss enjoying and benefiting from our talents in the workplace, our love and guidance within our families, and our engagement in our communities to the fullest extent possible. What a loss, and it need not be that way!

This part of the book moves through how Disability Inclusion benefits everyone, especially in the workplace. The purpose of these inclusive principles is to serve as a guide as to how everyone, including people with disabilities, must be afforded equal opportunities.

From there, I will lean mightily into the power of disability entrepreneurship and its importance in our world today and the opportunities it affords people with disabilities. As business owners, people with disabilities can enjoy greater control and choices in their lives, earn a good living, and encourage other people with disabilities to pursue entrepreneurship as well. Employers who buy from disability-diverse suppliers add immensely to the economic viability of entrepreneurship of people with disabilities.

For there to be a change in the workplace of today, there must be a much better understanding of how people with disabilities play an essential role in the Diversity, Equity, and Inclusion (DEI) movement. I explore how implementing DEI in the workplace impacts *all* employers and *all* employees.

Finally, I share my thoughts on how inclusive design significantly enables the workplace of the future. This important model should be used to make spaces usable and accessible for all.

1 Disability Inclusion Benefits Everyone

How many times a day do you ask Siri or Alexa to look something up for you? Send a text? How about asking it to play music? If you're like me, it's multiple times a day. The convenience of hands-free technology has exponentially made my life easier. Ever use a cart at the grocery store or at the airport? Curb cuts indeed make lugging those things around more maneuverable. They also help parents with strollers and kids and adults on bikes and scooters. Many of the things we use to simplify or quicken daily tasks were initially designed for disability access. Our complex and busy lives become more manageable and enjoyable when they are designed for all cases. Disability Inclusion benefits everyone.

I am a person who wears four artificial limbs, as I was born without most of my arms and legs. I've used prostheses since I was two years of age and my only childhood recollection is putting on my prostheses in the morning and wanting to get them off as quickly as possible in the evening! I definitely needed them to function as independently as possible.

When you think of physical spaces, what do you notice? I look for a combination of aesthetics and functionality. I want to feel welcomed, that I belong there. Whether I'm going some-place with a clear purpose in mind or wandering for leisure, I hope to enjoy the experience. Beyond the aesthetics, one key element I hope for is ease of use. How easy is it for me to do what I wanted to do? Do I feel comfortable and safe? How navigable is the space, meaning, how easy is it for me to find my way around? If architects designed the area well, I'll likely enjoy myself, and many others will, too.

John Stuart Mill's ethical philosophy declaration on Utilitarianism states:

> Utility, or the Greatest Happiness Principle, holds that actions are right in proportion as they tend to promote happiness, wrong as they tend to produce the reverse of happiness.

> —Mill [1863] 2017

Mill had a strong starting point but lost me when he argued that the majority rule would guarantee overall social success. As we witness the present day and look to the future, should we not ask ourselves how to include everyone? Nobody should be left behind if we genuinely believe in equity. So, how can we do that?

For one, if we plan to build structures with the most human factors in mind, it is likely they will be usable by most people in most scenarios. In other words, accessibility design and Disability Inclusion can benefit everyone because it reminds us to consider circumstances outside the median range of practical use and a broader view of human function. Logically, universal design, inclusive design, and accessibility principles make spaces, products, and services more functional and enjoyable for a significant percentage of people and less likely to be exclusionary.

As its name implies, universal design is for everyone. It was a good friend of mine, Ron Mace, now deceased, who founded the National Center of Barrier-Free Design at North Carolina State University, and created the concept of universal design founded on seven basic principles. These are:

1. Equitable Use
2. Flexibility in Use
3. Simple and Intuitive Use
4. Perceptible Information
5. Tolerance for Error
6. Low Physical Effort
7. Size and Space for Approach and Use

The purpose behind these guiding principles is that people of any ability should have identical or nearly equivalent operability and ease of use (Mace, Connell, Jones, et al. 1997; NDA 2020). If things are easy to use and functional for everyone, fewer problems arise. That's because when people can go about their day in the way that best fits their needs, our citizenry are generally more productive and happier.

Let's start with **equitable use**. A building, product, or website should be appealing and functional for all. The experience should be equally pleasant. When we consider dimensional space and manageable design aesthetics, people can do what they need and do it comfortably. The second principle, **flexibility in use**, expands on this idea by giving people options to use something. Preferential use such as left- or right-handedness is one example. Adjustment to a user's pace is another.

And the third, **simple and intuitive use**, makes the design easy to comprehend, regardless of the person's skill set. It should be consistent, clear, and manageable (Mace, Connell, Jones, et al. 1997; NDA 2020). These first three principles are beneficial for all people because they acknowledge that users are diverse. They may have different levels of technical or mechanical experience. They may need settings set at certain levels and consistently to complete tasks. They may speak or read other languages or have different reading levels.

Principles four, five, six, and seven are more targeted for variance in physicality. **Perceptible information** must be provided in several modalities, ranging from aural or visual to tactile. **Tolerance for error** allows users to get positive outcomes even when they make mistakes or misunderstand, provide safety of use, and warn users of hazards. Accidents happen, and people shouldn't have to suffer for them. The final two principles, **low physical effort** and **size and space for approach and use**, are probably the most recognizable. They are how most people understand the Americans with Disabilities Act. These principles guarantee that elements are accessible regardless of mobility, physical strength, height, posture, and endurance. These round out the experience by minimizing frustrating, repetitive gestures or commands, placing objects or buttons in comfortable locations, and allowing room for or pairing with accessible technologies (Mace, Connell, Jones, et al. 1997; NDA 2020).

There are other benefits beyond the physical and mental benefits for ease of use. Emotionally, we all feel and do our best when acknowledged, respected, and included. In the workplace, people with disabilities bring in a vast market of talent, innovation, and engagement. The potential of this untapped resource is invigorating for creative vision. That's something to look forward to as we seek to engage the public. On a more fundamental level, Disability Inclusion provides an opportunity to update workplace practices. Invigorating a workspace with disability diversity enriches corporate culture.

People with disabilities are not only a large consumer market. They are also a large pool of talent that's terribly underutilized.

Everyone benefits from the experiences of people with disabilities. You may learn that people with disabilities find novel approaches to problem solving because of daily practice adapting to other people and the environment. Diversity can lead others to adopt and encourage honesty in expression, foster openness in experimentation, and explore unconventional and exciting ideas. Fresh perspectives and behaviors are highly beneficial for collective workspace and community creativity.

Hannah Barham-Brown explained the complexity and importance of Disability Inclusion in the workforce in her 2019 TED Talk "Disability and Work: Let's Stop Wasting Talent." After telling her personal story about being a doctor living with a disability, she emphasized that Disability Inclusion is more important than ticking boxes on the diversity checklist. Rather than viewing diversity hires as hitting a symbolic goal, though a "safeguard" for the disability community, the focus needs to be on the richness of the disability lived experience. She told her audience:

> Every job advert you see will say that a company is looking for problem solvers, people who think outside the box, great "team workers." Well, we are nature's problem solvers because we live in a world that was designed without us in mind. (Barham-Brown 2019)

She emphasized that because of the survival need to adapt, many people with disabilities are good with team interaction; we learn to communicate our needs and assess roles best suited for peers. She continues, "What we have to bring is exciting, is under-recognized, and woefully underutilized. We do so much more than tick a diversity box" (Barham-Brown 2019).

What potential is unleashed when we move beyond disability survival? People with disabilities already have developed skill sets that set us apart from peers and highlight our value, and that is while trying to survive in difficult, inaccessible settings. When we remove barriers, potential becomes actualized.

Statistics echo Barham-Brown's sentiment about underutilized talent. The CDC (2020) estimates that about 61 million people in the United States and more than a billion worldwide are living with a disability. The Bureau of Labor Statistics (2022) released data highlighting that "[a]cross all age groups, persons with disabilities were much less likely to be employed than those with no disabilities," and that in 2020, "the unemployment rate for persons with a disability increased 5.3% points from the previous year." There is much potential in this talent pool now that is underrepresented and often excluded altogether. When people are employed, they revitalize the economy. They also strengthen the workforce. Ideally, employment helps expand and nurture neighborhood development both residentially and commercially and, when people put efforts into diversity and inclusion, it enriches the arts and local culture.

When workspaces, public spaces, and governments commit to accessibility and inclusion of people with disabilities, it sends the message that multiple voices and differences are accepted and valued. Not everyone will be open about disability disclosure, and some people may benefit from accessible practices but not identify as having a disability. Designing for the "fringes" of human variance broadens the scope and provides coverage for the unrepresented or "invisible." Even people without disabilities benefit from an array of options. For example, some people prefer reading in a larger font or listening to audio rather than reading long documents. Assistive technologies provide opportunities for people to streamline and personalize their workflow and enhance productivity.

Furthermore, spaces and practices that present flexibility, comfort, and inclusion will keep people around. People respond well to seeing themselves represented and considered.

People with disabilities are a large population—with a somewhat difficult universe of people with disabilities to measure, as different federal agencies use different definitions and some people with hidden disabilities that require no care or services are not counted at all. The size can vary from the Centers for Disease Control and Prevention (CDC) estimating approximately 1 in 4 people has a disability in the United States (CDC, 2020) to 41.1 million or 12.7% of the total civilian noninstitutionalized population with a disability in the United States in 2019 (https://www.census.gov/newsroom/facts-for-features/2021/disabilities-act.html). By the way, the total institutionalized population in 2020 was 1.5 million people (https://www.census.gov/library/stories/2021/08/united-states-group-quarters-in-2020-census.html).

It makes economic and communal sense to appeal favorably to an untapped resource and market. Companies may experience lower turnover rates and higher employee morale in the workforce. Employees who feel protected, respected, and appreciated stay. In 1943, Abraham H. Maslow presented a Humanistic Theory of motivation based on a hierarchy of five essential needs people experience. Our **physiological** and **safety** needs are at the base, including the human drives for food and shelter. Next are emotional needs, such as **love or belonging**, **esteem** (status), and **self-actualization** (Maslow [1943] 2011). In survival mode, employees work out of necessity. They need to feel the body's safety, health, family/community, access to resources, and ownership (Maslow [1943] 2011). If basic worker needs are monetary compensation, health benefits, and accessibility, then the companies must take steps and initiatives to make employees feel they belong. Employees who have their basic needs met can focus on higher objectives personally and professionally. Confidence and morale go a long way in enhancing motivation and collective success.

Whether or not this is apparent or subconscious, it applies to public perception overall. Companies that respect workers and care about Diversity, Equity, and Inclusion (DEI), which MUST include disability, tend to fare better with public image and consumer satisfaction. Companies may also experience greater brand loyalty and financial backing when investing in social justice projects. Disability Inclusion helps with marketing and media representation and overall publicity. And that publicity can, in turn, improve outcomes for people with disabilities if the messaging is respectful by helping to redefine the public's attitudes regarding disability.

Tailoring educational, organizational, or commercial needs to diverse populations also has large-scale effects. Providing safe housing, employment, and personal growth opportunities by including disability is a return on investment because it strengthens neighborhoods, promotes social harmony, lowers poverty, and serves the public good. We can only combat bias and stigma when expanding who we include in political discourse. Disability Inclusion benefits everyone because it provides another lens in the DEI movement that can enhance workplace ingenuity, communication skills, and camaraderie.

When culture accepts and encourages your identity, nobody can tell you that you cannot be who you want or where you must place yourself in the world. This is well addressed by a dear friend of mine, Caroline Casey of Ireland, a powerful global voice of Disability Inclusion. To raise awareness of disability as a common characteristic that should be accepted rather than avoided, she's ridden an elephant across India and hosted a televised corporate awards program honoring Ireland's best companies for their Disability Inclusion.

More recently, she's been developing relationships with the world's top corporate leaders in Davos, Switzerland, at the annual World Economic Forum. From these relationships she created The Valuable 500, a strong program engaging top corporate global leaders pledging to advance an agenda of Disability Inclusion and who are willing to be held accountable for their successes and failures.

In her TED Talk, she beautifully connects Maslow's hierarchy of needs with disability identity and culture. In "Looking Past Limits," Caroline Casey emphasized the importance of disability confidence, belonging, and self-actualization in success and morale (2010). She started her story by reminiscing about how we dream as children. We are unaware of our limits because of our innocence. The world has not told us who it thinks we are yet. Caroline said that when people started to use her diagnosis of limited sight to dismiss her capabilities, her response became to prove them wrong by showing herself as just as talented and worthy.

The turning point in her narrative came at 28 years old, when she was struggling to do her job. She faced disclosing her legal blindness to the human resources department (Casey 2010). This moment underscored a few important things worth noting. While not the focus of Caroline's narrative, this story highlights the need for inclusive practices in someone's professional and personal life from a workplace perspective. A welcoming environment and inclusive practices benefit the entire organization because asking for help can be intimidating for many, regardless of disability status.

For example, in the United States and the United Kingdom, culturally, people are expected to be independent and self-sufficient.

This is especially true in a high-intensity workplace. Human resources and organizations can reduce feelings of stress and anxiety and promote mental health simply by providing a setting where workers can express their needs.

Having fought against the stream for years to pass as a seeing person, Caroline faced a difficult choice. There were a few realizations for her. One was that her chosen field of work was not accessible for her. Secondly, she had chosen work that did not encourage or sustain her happiness; she decided on a career she felt proved she was just like everybody else. The disclosure and its impact led her to make a career change (Casey 2010). She looked back on when she was a child before the world told her what she could or could not be and used that knowledge to influence her future career. She chose work that mattered to her and goals that mattered to her. Her company lost an employee because the space wasn't accessible and wasn't providing fulfillment, and her future led her to more meaningful work anyway. She gave back to her community and encouraged confidence and inclusion practices. She concluded her TED Talk with the statement,

> And if you truly believe—and I mean believe from the bottom of your heart—you can make change happen. And we need to make it happen, because every single one of us—woman, man, gay, straight, disabled, perfect, normal, whatever—every one of us must be the very best of ourselves. I no longer want anybody to be invisible. We all have to be included. And stop with the labels, the limiting. Losing of labels, because we are not jam jars. We are extraordinary, different, wonderful people. (Casey 2010)

It is essential to recognize that while disability identity is vital for access to accommodations, labels do not have to be limiting. The purpose of disclosure in a workplace or social setting should be to access services and accommodations that empower and liberate all of us, including people with disabilities. When we include disability in the cultural sphere, we provide more opportunities and tap into valuable skills, experiences, and talent. Disability Inclusion benefits everyone because it helps us design for the unexpected. It helps us learn adaptability. It helps us all to think about ways to go beyond limitations and expectations. It encourages us to get creative, break the status quo, and experiment. Then, together, we can innovate and grow exponentially.

2 The Power of Disability Entrepreneurship

The time is ripe for the encouragement of people with disabilities to become entrepreneurs, and to address and remove daunting additional barriers facing potential entrepreneurs who have disabilities. Archaic public policies, disability discrimination in the workplace and people with disabilities becoming so psychologically and completely discouraged from work all throw tremendous adverse barriers in front of adults with disabilities. Entrepreneurship becomes for many, the only viable alternative to living a life with some dignity intact. What other group of citizens faces such choices?

Becoming an entrepreneur must be a free, knowledgeable, enlightened career choice, where adults make serious commitments to risking their reputations, their meager resources, and what they've managed to cobble together from family and friends. I admire any adult with a disability who dares to take on this challenge, and this is but one reason that The Viscardi Center in Albertson, New York, and I, while serving as its president and CEO, began the National Center for Disability Entrepreneurship. Formed in 2017, the center provides resources, bridges to funders and experts, and even small financial support to budding entrepreneurs with disabilities.

Disabled adults ready to explore entrepreneurship face serious policy barriers in the form of Social Security's current limits on asset accumulation (approximately $2,000 total as of 2022), a level which has been set and not moved for more than 20 years. If a disabled person accumulates assets exceeding $2,000, our US Social Security Administration presumes this person has sufficient assets and that no SSA benefits are needed. This is an absurd outcome and without SSA indexing this number and increasing it substantially, it seriously limits economic opportunities for self-employment and thwarts one of the fundamental promises of the 1990 Americans with Disabilities Act, i.e. economic independence.

Add to this major barrier in federal public policy the significant disparity in labor force participation rates between disabled adults of working age and adults without disabilities of working age, a disparity of more than 41.4%, with only 35.1% of disabled adults participating in the workforce versus nearly 76.5% of adults without disabilities.

According to the University of New Hampshire's Center on Disability, in partnership with the esteemed Kessler Institute on Rehabilitation, disabled adults over the past three calendar years, 2019–2021, have been quite resilient in regaining lost ground in employment, though the numbers and percentages remain woefully low:

> At the start of 2022, as the acute phase of the COVID-19 pandemic began to subside and public health efforts continued, experts reflected on the pandemic's impact on employment in the U.S. This [March 2022] special edition of National Trends in Disability Employment (nTIDE) presents data from 2019 through 2021 for people with and without disabilities, showing stark contrasts in their progression from pre-pandemic employment levels of 2019, the impact of 2020 lockdowns, followed by the beginnings of recovery in 2021. (Kessler Foundation and UNH 2022)

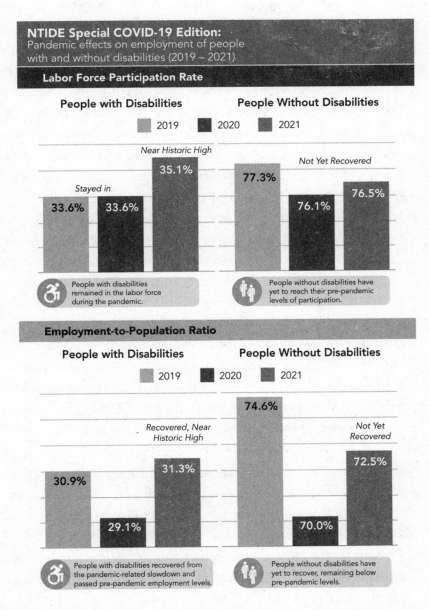

FIGURE 2.1 Employment Indicators for People with and Without Disabilities

Source: Kessler Foundation and the University of New Hampshire Institute on Disability. National Trends in Disability Employment Report (nTIDE). 2022.

Figure 2.1 compares employment indicators for people with and without disabilities from 2019 to 2021, showing people with disabilities have recovered from pandemic lows and exceeded pre-pandemic employment levels, while people without disabilities have yet to recover.

The data show that people with disabilities have not only recovered from the setbacks of 2020 lockdowns, but they have also exceeded pre-pandemic levels of employment to reach new historic highs. This contrasts with their counterparts without disabilities who have yet to reach their pre-pandemic levels of employment.

As the top graphic shows, in 2019 and 2020, the labor force participation rate remained the same for people with disabilities (33.6%), rising to 35.1% in 2021. "Despite the disruption of the pandemic, people with disabilities stayed engaged in the labor market, meaning they were working, on furlough, or looking for work," explained nTIDE co-author Andrew Houtenville, PhD, professor of economics and research director of the University of New Hampshire Institute on Disability. In 2021, participation rose above pre-pandemic levels to 35.1%, exceeding the historic high seen in 2008 around the start of the Great Recession. "This may be a sign that people with disabilities are taking advantage of new job opportunities in the tight labor market," added Dr. Houtenville. "Necessity may also be a factor in sustained participation, as workers with disabilities may be less able to forego their income."

For people without disabilities, labor force participation rate dropped from 77.3% in 2019 to 76.1% in 2020, rising to 76.5% in 2021, still well below pre-pandemic levels. "They are returning slowly to the labor market," noted Dr. Houtenville, "and have yet to recover the ground they lost in 2020."

In the bottom graphic, the comparison of employment to population ratios tells a similar story of resilience. In 2019, the employment population ratio was 30.9% for people with disabilities, dropping to 29.1% in 2020, then surpassing pre-pandemic levels, rising to 31.3% in 2021. "Again, not only did people with disabilities recover, but they also exceeded their pre-pandemic levels, approaching historic highs." In contrast, the employment-to-population ratio for people without disabilities declined from 74.6% in 2019 to 70.0% in 2020, reaching only 72.5% in 2021.

These stark contrasts are fascinating findings, according to nTIDE co-author John O'Neill, PhD, director of the Center for Employment and Disability Research at Kessler Foundation. "It really is a story of true grit. On the whole, despite the stresses of the pandemic, people with disabilities stayed in the labor force, a pattern we hope to see continue as the pandemic evolves," he emphasized. "It's also crucial that we ensure that the hard-won gains achieved by workers with disabilities are sustainable as people without disabilities continue to return to the labor force. That will require concerted efforts by advocates, workers, employers, vocational rehabilitation professionals, and other stakeholders." (Kessler Foundation and UNH 2022)

While, as a society, we believe that government is a safety net and its benefits are to be used as a last resort, current public policy forces many people with disabilities into an underground economy and to live constructed lives of, for example, no marriage (marriage draws a possibly eligible person with a disability into having to claim their spouse's assets in a combined means test, which could disqualify an otherwise qualified SSA beneficiary from receiving SSA benefits).

Today, with social and economic barriers strictly and unfairly limiting people with disabilities to attempt entrepreneurship, it's not in the public's interest to keep creative, innovative disabled people out of the economic mainstream and dependent on the public for their mere subsistence. Just using an investment theory, public monies invested in entrepreneurs with disabilities could yield fantastic double-net gains for our public coffers: (1) removing people from the Social Security roles, and (2) creating tax-generating businesses and individual taxpayers.

In my opinion, the time has come to unleash the inner entrepreneur in people with disabilities by resolving this big policy barrier plus the barriers of unequal access to capital and credit facing millions of people with disabilities.

Entrepreneurship, according to the US Internal Revenue Service, is the act of generating one's own income through a business as opposed to being an employee in a business. Any person is considered self-employed if they are running a business as (a) a sole proprietor, (b) an independent contractor, (c) a member of a partnership, (d) a member of a limited liability company that does not elect to be treated as a corporation, (e) a member of a business cooperative, or (f) a freelancer.

Whether "entrepreneurs are born or made" is a long-standing debate around the world. Many business owners agree they are born with some traits that help them be successful in a competitive market and that leadership and willingness to take risks are some of the entrepreneurial traits that are acquired at birth. Individuals with these innate traits can become successful entrepreneurs in the competitive world through training or experience in the key aspects of business and investment. On the other hand, a central key to the success of start-ups is a good quality business plan.

Writing a business plan forces potential entrepreneurs to focus on the important and essential elements of their business. It makes them think through the next steps and specific strategies and tactics; but most importantly, the process forces entrepreneurs to learn the facts of the business, such as the potential market, the product or service, the financing, and the organizational, legal and management structures of the proposed business. Planning these aspects help the entrepreneur to determine the feasibility and implementation of the business idea. A quality business plan is also required for any potential investor to consider financing the venture.

Has a prolonged adult existence on disability-dependency payments reduced such recipients' ability to write smart, focused, crisp business plans? Hardly, and only in some instances. That's where The Viscardi Center's National Center for Disability Entrepreneurship comes into play—a very important play.

Economists have argued that well-established firms could actually be considered job-destroyers leading to the loss of approximately 1 million jobs per year for 21 out of the 28 years between 1977 and 2005. Conversely, for the same time period, start-ups added around 3 million new jobs to the American economy in their first year of operation. So not only does self-employment and entrepreneurship have the potential to positively impact the lives of people with disabilities, it could also help the overall economy. However, this is by no means a miracle cure for unemployment. Entrepreneurship is a risky endeavor, with 75% of all venture-backed start-ups failing after the first year (Ghosh 2012).

The US Department of Labor's Bureau of Labor Statistics (BLS) explained that most new businesses fail because the owners do not see beyond their initial ideas and they lack the experience and/or expertise needed to run a successful business. Business survival, however, varies by industry, with the health care and social service industries consistently ranking among those with the highest survival rates over time, while construction ranks among the lowest.

Development of a business plan should include:
a. products and services to be offered;
b. defining the market for one's products and services;
c. the accurate identification of one's competition;

d. the elements and costs in a marketing and sales plan;

e. the entrepreneur's planned business operations;

f. the business's management structure;

g. possible scenarios regarding future developments; and,

h. the business's plans for financing itself over time.

Are the Odds Stacked Against People with Disabilities Becoming Entrepreneurs?

It is well understood that people with disabilities are less likely to be gainfully employed and will have lower earnings than nondisabled people. These differentials are caused by a variety of factors, including perceived and actual discrimination.

As an alternative career option for people with disabilities, being self-employed can yield the benefits of the freedom, flexibility, and independence associated with self-employment, as well as autonomy from access-related obstacles such as transportation, fatigue, inaccessible work environments, and the need for personal assistance. However, people with disabilities who are considering establishing their own business face many barriers—which a nondisabled person will not endure—and they therefore require additional supports and services.

Over the past two decades, the term "entrepreneurship" has received ever-increasing levels of media and government attention. The primary reason for such attention is the well-documented evidence of the positive relationship between entrepreneurship and economic growth. It has therefore been in the best interests of a nation's economy for governments to engender an entrepreneurial culture that advances the development of indigenous enterprise, for example, and the promotion of individual "entrepreneurial heroes" within that culture furthers such a goal. The notion of the entrepreneur as the lone hero was initially fueled in the United States by stories of the meteoric careers of individuals such as Andrew Carnegie and John D. Rockefeller. This was because entrepreneurship is enmeshed in our historic culture and because American society encourages and promotes personal and singular achievement; thus, the lone entrepreneur reigns supreme. Small business owners are revered because of their symbolism of self-reliant personal independence. Because the United States greatly influences international opinion, other countries have generally conformed to this interpretation of an entrepreneur.

In more recent times, the concept of the entrepreneur has been explored more broadly and there is a growing body of literature that analyzes entrepreneurs from a wide variety of perspectives, particularly within a genre that has been termed "minority," "disadvantaged," or "marginalized" entrepreneurs. Chief among these has been female and ethnic entrepreneurs. Unfortunately, little has been written about entrepreneurs with disabilities (EWD). People with disabilities, like everyone else, seek and obtain qualifications and use them to gain employment and income. This partly contradicts the general impression of disability that instinctively implies that some form of social welfare and protection is the answer and that people with disabilities are unsuitable for serious business. This in turn leads to an apprehension about the ability of people with disabilities to establish a viable business. Reactions like, "It is hard enough for them to find jobs: how can they possibly create them?" not only show a lack of confidence in the capabilities of people with disabilities, but also reflect a typical view about self-employment being something that requires powers greater than the average person possesses. After the barrier of asset limits under Social Security, this is precisely the next greatest barrier to entrepreneurship for people with disabilities.

Any starting point regarding entrepreneurs with disabilities (EWDs) must first begin with a review of the general employment figures for people with disabilities as it sets an important context to the discussion. It is now widely recognized that having a disability has a negative effect upon rates of employment and earnings. Peter Blanck, a friend and professor, and his colleagues at Syracuse University, used the US Census Bureau's Current Population Survey from 20 years ago to identify that only 30.4% of people with a work disability between the ages of 16 and 64 were in the labor force, as opposed to 82.3% of nondisabled people in the same category. In 2022, those numbers have shifted slightly, with 35.1% of people with disabilities in the same age range employed and 76.5% of nondisabled adults in the same range in the labor force. Earnings were similarly unbalanced with the mean earnings for people with disabilities holding full-time jobs being $29,513, compared to $37,961 for nondisabled people, a drop of approximately 22%. In addition, they also found that people with disabilities had significantly lower levels of education. Nearly 31% of people with disabilities had not completed high school, while only 17.5% of nondisabled people had not done so, though this gap or disparity is narrowing each year. The study found that such lower levels of educational attainment understandably had a negative influence on the capacity of people with disabilities to secure good employment and earning opportunities.

A low level of educational attainment is one significant factor that influences the capacity of a disabled person to secure employment. But most people with disabilities acquire their disabilities well after birth.

Other factors affecting an individual's ability or willingness to supply their labor are likely to include: the severity of the disability, access to and within a potential workplace, beliefs about the likelihood of facing discrimination, and the trade-off between employment income and benefit receipts, which can include food stamps and critically necessary health care.

Interestingly, the personal experiences of employers who have a family member or friend who has a disability can have a positive influence on their willingness to offer a person with a disability competitive, integrated employment. However, more generally, mediating organizations play a pivotal role in providing assistance in terms of increasing awareness of the benefits of employing people with disabilities and in offering appropriate training support. While these mediating organizations struggle to cope with the enormous challenge they face in educating employers to change their behavior, some people with disabilities turn to self-employment as an alternative solution for generating income.

Entrepreneurship has been the default solution to workplace misery in gaining a decent job. Entrepreneurship should be an unfettered choice to pursue, and not the default, for people with pride, great work ethic, and drive. A great public policy framework would be for entrepreneurship and self-employment to be used more frequently to help people with disabilities to move from unemployment, underemployment, and welfare-based income to gainful employment and self-sufficiency.

People with disabilities have a higher rate of self-employment than people without disabilities, with approximately 40% of self-employed people with disabilities having home-based businesses. Of those, 14.6% of men with disabilities were self-employed, compared with 9.6% of men with no disabilities, while 9% of women with disabilities were self-employed, compared with 5.6% of women with no disabilities.

It has been suggested that people with disabilities make natural entrepreneurs because having a disability can also be a stimulus for independent problem solving and innovation. I know this to be true, personally. And children with disabilities often develop new and effective ways of moving around, communicating, or otherwise successfully managing the limitations of their disabilities. The experience of living with disabilities can be a valuable, though sometimes onerous, form of personal development.

As I've discussed, all too often the reasons people with disabilities start our own businesses are heavily rooted in negative motives. As with any new venture creation, the attitudes of the entrepreneur (with a disability or not) are more important than those of the general public when it comes to determining the viability of entrepreneurship as a choice. The concept of a businessperson is in definite contrast to the widespread image that many people with disabilities have of themselves: to have a right to necessary services if and when needed, to have others to make decisions on their behalf, and to wait for job opportunities rather than take the initiative in seeking employment. Furthermore, the attitudes of the very people whose job it is to assist people with disabilities may also be counter-productive to the promotion of self-employment.

There are, however, a number of positive factors that may make it easier, rather than harder, for some people with disabilities to survive in their own businesses. Indeed, very often it is the psychological condition of people with disabilities that makes them particularly likely to persevere in self-employment and to do well.

According to a 2001 US Department of Labor policy document, the benefits of a person with a disability operating a small business include freedom, flexibility, and independence associated with self-employment, and autonomy from access-related obstacles such as transportation, fatigue, inaccessible work environments, and the need for personal assistance.

Table 2.1   Getting Started: Why Did Respondents Choose Self-Employment?

1 Wanted to "work for myself"	56%
2 Identified need for product/service	48%
3 Wanted to make more money	46%
4 Wanted to own a business	46%
5 Needed to create own job	44%
6 To accommodate a disability (i.e. flexible hours and/or working conditions)	43%
7 Other jobs unavailable	15%

Source: APRIL. "Disability and Self-Employment, A Formula for Success." *Employment Brief* 4, no. 2. NTAC-AAPI. 2001.

A survey undertaken by APRIL, the Association of Programs for Rural Independent Living, in conjunction with the Disabled Businesspersons Association, found that the principal reason disabled people gave for starting a business was because they wanted to work for themselves. Table 2.1 highlights the findings regarding why people with disabilities choose self-employment. It is interesting to note that the reasons given are primarily positive.

Similar to the results found in Table 2.1, British researchers Melanie Jones and Paul Latreille offered data signifying that self-employment is due to the greater flexibility in hours and times afforded in self-employment, and that the higher rates of self-employment among people with disabilities reflects a voluntary choice that best accommodates the limitations of their disability. However, these findings are in contrast with much of the other research that has sought to identify the central motives that people with disabilities tendered for starting their own business. For example, Peter Blanck et al. (2001) highlighted the role of disability discrimination, either perceived or actual, as a major motivation and concluded that self-employment offered increased employment opportunities for people with disabilities. Likewise, Rutgers University Professor Lisa Schur, also a friend, found that disability discrimination was an important explanation of the higher rates of self-employment that are to be found among people with disabilities than among nondisabled people. As can be seen, authors such as Blanck et al. and Schur believe that, while there are many positive reasons for people with disabilities establishing their own business, prejudice and other negative motivations remain the key initiating factors.

As with all forms of entrepreneurship, there are "push" and "pull" factors influencing the decision to start one's own business. Undoubtedly, the discrimination faced by people with disabilities in terms of employment and earnings opportunities encourages many to become self-employed. But frequently self-employment is also a lifestyle choice that offers people with disabilities the freedom to work at their own pace in an environment that accommodates their particular needs. Owning our own business also provides people with disabilities the flexibility that is necessary for those who may require more frequent medical attention, flexible hours, accessible workspace, and/or other considerations. Whatever the motives for starting the business, the higher rates of self-employment among our disability community require that when people with disabilities do look to start their own business, the appropriate support is available to help them with the process.

"Entrepreneurship" is a dangerously fashionable term, and many governments and others are grasping at the concept of "enterprise" as a solution to their economic difficulties. Only a minority of any given population is likely to possess the necessary desire to start and sustain their own enterprise and the position of people with disabilities is no different. Self-employment is not a panacea through which all people with disabilities can become self-supporting and circumvent the low rates of employment and income we currently experience. While some may be pushed into self-employment because their disability may disqualify them from other forms of livelihood, or real disability discrimination forces many of us to start our own business, entrepreneurship should be just as valid a choice or option as it is for nondisabled people.

It is, of course, impossible to state what proportion of people with disabilities may reasonably be considered as potential entrepreneurs. Quite contrary to common prejudice, which tends to associate certain disabilities with certain jobs, it is an established principle that each case requires individual assessment. This clearly means that the feasibility of a self-employment venture can be determined only when taking into account the circumstances of the individual. Not only does one's disability count as an important factor in assessing one's suitability for self-employment but even more critical is their surrounding environment (e.g. the availability and affordability of housing, health care, accessible public transportation, and the extent to which the community's built environment is itself accessible). Successful self-employment will also depend on whether the person has the necessary combination of personal and professional characteristics to make them an entrepreneur. Tailored approaches offer the most appropriate and most effective method of supporting those people with disabilities who wish to establish their own business.

Entrepreneurship is oftentimes the consequence of workplace discrimination with extremely limited choices for people with disabilities. Rather than choosing to sit at home and live on subsistence-level incomes with food stamps and other benefits, entrepreneurship is often a last resort. If we take away the last resort of entrepreneurship, we are left as a society with the high cost of disability exclusion, which benefits no one.

What Is the High Cost of Disability Exclusion?

Often cited as the largest minority group, it is estimated that persons with disabilities compose upwards of 15% of the world's population, or nearly 1 billion people (United Nations Division for Social Policy and Development n.d.). What is commonly overlooked, however, is the degree of diversity within the disability community. Persons with disabilities are the only group that represents the full breadth of intersectional identities of human beings. Although persons with disabilities are commonly thought of as a homogenous, monolithic group, across our community, we see the intersection of age, cultural background, disability type, economic situation, educational attainment level, gender, geographic influence, race, religion, and sexual orientation.

The failure to recognize the diversity of our community, in terms of data collection, the formation of business strategies, and the adoption of inclusive public policies, is a critical factor in the global loss of productivity and innovation. Even as public awareness of Disability Inclusion elevates in society's consciousness, disability issues remain an afterthought. Rather than considering the disability community when policies, practices, and procedures are first developed, access issues are often remedied with amendments and apologies. This reality is continuously reinforced by reports of global trends in lower educational attainment and employment, along with higher rates of poverty among people with disabilities.

The Personal Costs of Exclusion

The exclusion of persons with disabilities contributes to the lost potential of millions of people and their contributions to everyone's quality of life. Denying and discouraging hundreds of millions of people with disabilities—with arbitrary, thoughtless, and exclusionary policies—from full participation in all aspects of society is as base and disgusting, short of disability genocide, as society can be. While we people with disabilities generally live very unfulfilled lives, it is society that pays the price of exclusion, i.e. all of us. We can't achieve the highest levels **we** choose, we can't give our best efforts, and we're not afforded the highest level of learning. We can't create the greatest innovations possible or become extraordinary entrepreneurs simply because the policies of exclusion allow it to continue. Consider the waste and underdevelopment of talent that occurs because we don't think and act inclusively.

Think about the policies in place (or not) and how they could impact your life. What if:

- At your birth or shortly thereafter, a health crisis arose, and decisions had to be made as to whether "costs of emergency medical care would be a considerable factor" to save your life or save certain bodily functions. You survived but have serious residual limitations, physically or mentally, or both. Would the willingness to spend money have kept you from acquiring a disability with serious limitations? I don't know. But, I do know that poor, uninsured people using the Medicaid system as their backstop do not have access to the resources that privately insured people receive. There are cost decisions made every day and everywhere about how much professional medical services and technologies will be devoted to helping a pregnant woman deliver the healthiest baby possible, and "medicine" errs too often on the side of not committing to providing all the available resources that are available.

- When you reach school age, depending on your disability, you are designated as needing special education services and an annual Individualized Education Plan (IEP). It is developed, mutually agreed on by your school district and your parents, and implemented precisely. You will always be a "special ed" student, and rarely, if ever, will you have that label removed. While it assures you of fundamental rights and legal protections, it can be as stigmatizing as anything you'll face.

- The disability you have means your family members become your attendants and only well-balanced individuals and families learn how to deliver and receive personal, intimate supports and services while maintaining a healthy parent-child relationship. Is that you and your family? Having a non-family member providing personal care services is invaluable to maintaining a strong, balanced parent-child relationship.

- As a high schooler, are you afforded the socialization, academic, and after-school opportunities, or their equivalents, that are afforded all students? You are continually striving to fight your way into these programs and activities as opposed to presumptively belong to them.

- If your limitations involve speech or mobility, what equivalent activities is your school providing you, like wheelchair basketball or debate or STEM programs? You say, "There are no equivalent or nearly equivalent programs." Welcome to our world.

- Pick a college or two. Are they accessible physically, programmatically, and with accessible information and communication technologies (ICT) that meet your individual needs? Or do you "choose" to live at home for the personal care and support, while missing the dorm all-nighters and the once in a while wild and crazy spontaneous drinking party scenes?

- Assuming you are among the minority of disabled college students who ultimately graduate from a four-year school, do you stay in the "safe place" of college (because you've worked out your personal attendant services under Medicaid, probably) and keep going for an advanced degree, or do you dare to venture out to look for paid employment?
- You choose to seek paid work, knowing the employment rate for persons with disabilities is only up 1% since the Americans with Disabilities Act's (ADA) passage in 1990. You're faced with the dilemma of self-identifying that you have a disability because you need a "reasonable accommodation" in the pre-employment phase, something you disclose in response to pre-employment inquiries suggests you have a disability ("received vocational rehabilitation services scholarship to help pay for college"), or you refuse to disclose it and work around the pre-employment barriers. Good idea, or not?
- After you apply online, you are sent a list of seven questions that you must answer in video format and submit via an online corporate/employer portal. Artificial Intelligence (AI) will analyze all video responses from applicants as well as everyone's résumé, and AI will determine whether you conform logarithmically within an acceptable range of job qualifications for the job in question. This is then compared with who else is in the employer's AI database, and that's usually their previously hired employees. If your limitation (or intersectionality, or your culture) causes you difficulty in establishing or maintaining eye contact with the camera, or your voice or voice

output is too slow or too fast, or you stutter, chances are great that the AI will remove you from the applicant pool that's moved forward.

- You've made it through the applicant process to where you've been invited for an in-person interview. You know your disability will become apparent to the interviewer(s), and now you must decide how to disclose and maintain that you are "job-qualified." Do you know what the daily job tasks are so you can determine if you'll need a reasonable accommodation? Probably not yet. Do you know how you'll get from home to work, via mass transit or your car, and how you'll move from drop-off spot or parking space to your office/cubicle? Again, not yet. Remember, you have hardly begun to climb the competency curve of your job following your initial hire, with almost your entire reason for being hired—to perform a job—still in front of you! And, you are most anxious about being able to demonstrate your competency all the while managing the disability aspects surrounding your employment.

- You've made it past the first 90 days in your new job, the usual probationary or trial period of employment, wherein the employer can deem you "a poor fit" or use almost any loosely job-related reason to terminate your employment. Maybe you've made it through your first full year of employment and you're a proven, competent employee. Are you included in company-sponsored events, like on- and off-site trainings, the annual picnic, the holiday party, etc.? Is company information delivered in an accessible way, or does the employer make a "big deal" about having to make a separate set of materials for *you*? Are events *always* held in physically accessible places? If not, is the eye-rolling so "loud" that you are perceived as the "whiner" and you are being passively ostracized, and thus slowly alienated from the bigger group? We know these micro-communications occur, and without being "paranoid," everybody, including you, know that *you* are a pain to include, as you "always need something special, just for you alone."

- You have a social life away from work. Where do you meet someone if it's not through work? Do you spend your life hanging out in bars, waiting for the right person to come along? Hopefully not, but sometimes. Your friends usually would try to introduce you to a good person. Are they forewarning that person about your disability? Yes, probably. You'll pray that having a disability is not a deciding factor in whether a potential date would predetermine they don't want to go out with you. Then, nature takes hold, as in any relationship.

As you have read earlier, I've been blessed by finding and marrying the love of my life, Sam. She was never daunted by my having a disability or frustrated by the limitations it silently may have caused her, I'm sure, to be able to do things together. When there was something she wanted to do that I would have trouble doing, we talked about it. I always encouraged her to go with a friend or a family member, but not to stop wanting to do it simply because I couldn't enjoy it with her. May everyone find someone as loving and open-minded as I found in Sam.

Possibly to your surprise, most disabled people don't find their mate as someone living with a disability. Age or accident or illness may visit a nondisabled partner, and the couple may become a couple where both of whom are living with disabilities. But, in my anecdotal analysis, most disabled people find life partners with nondisabled people who might well acquire a disability along life's path.

By charting this "through the eyes of a person with a disability from birth" experience, I want you to feel the stigma, the inaccessibility, and sometimes downright thoughtlessness we face every day. At times, it's beyond belief how poorly we are treated and the barriers of all kinds we face. No one has ever said to me, "I wish we could trade places." Maybe they might want to change places for the professional opportunities I've created for myself and with Sam's amazing support, or for those I have been given, or for the great person I married, or for only a short period of time. Our lives are just as fulfilling as those of nondisabled people but it's mostly because we have found ways to correct injustices appropriately, changes policies and practices accordingly, and obtain reasonable accommodations that are understandably necessary to make work opportunities fair and just.

I have too much respect for myself and my life's efforts to create equality, equity, and fairness for all people that I will not share myself with people and organizations that don't share that same respect for me or people with disabilities, period.

But, there are broader, deeper social/societal reasons, economic and even political reasons that Disability Inclusion is an imperative that can be ignored no longer.

General Societal Costs of Exclusion

We also see the social cost of exclusion in reinforced stigmas and discrimination, dependency on others, and increased pressure placed on caregivers and public systems, as well as the residual health impacts associated with poverty (Kanady, Muncie, and Missimer 2020).

Fundamentally, such issues originate from the social identity of persons with disabilities that are held by others and projected on the community or internalized due to a lifetime of experiencing discrimination. Society fails to place equal value on persons with disabilities and their nondisabled peers. This reality becomes even more complicated when we recognize the diverse intersection of identities with the persons within the community, and the additional barriers associated with age, gender, and race. The undervaluing of persons with disabilities is a root cause for underinvestment in education and workforce development programs that leads to the many problematic outcomes identified throughout this post.

Individuals, firms, and nations can begin to assess their behaviors and act toward positive change by recognizing the role that social identity–based barriers play in excluding persons with disabilities. As a social construct, this can be aided by addressing how persons with disabilities are depicted as either sympathetic, charitable caricatures, as heroes overcoming adversity, or as a population to avoid due to cultural biases. Disability is a part of the human experience that is likely to touch everyone's life in some way. If we don't become fully inclusive, we fail to recognize their humanity and exclude people with disabilities from fully contributing to society, to the detriment of everyone.

Political Costs of Exclusion

While the economic cost of exclusion is well documented, the political costs are more nuanced. We view the political costs as the by-product of policy and regulatory actions that fail to achieve their intended outcomes or that create unintended consequences.

It is understood that the adoption of universal design or universal access principles can lead to significant cost savings and downstream benefits in the areas of construction and technology development (Wentz, Jaeger, and Lazar 2011; Fuglerud,

Hallbach, and Tjostheim 2015). The same can be said for policymaking. By directly including the disability community in the design of education, employment, social welfare, and technology policies, governments worldwide could avoid the costly duplication of efforts related to amendments or stand-alone legislation that attempt to correct unintended exclusion. This requires a recognition of persons with disabilities as students, taxpayers, and vital contributors to the workforce instead of their usual depiction as just beneficiaries of social programs.

From a regulatory standpoint, we see the political costs as the interaction between compulsory action, free will, and unencumbered market activity. When government seeks to correct a known issue with regulatory frameworks, it can lead to a range of unintended responses. This includes avoidance, increased fear of legal consequences, and underperformance relative to goals. A specific example is the enforcement of employment quotas for public and private sector hiring of persons with disabilities in some countries around the world. Rather than address the root-cause issues of stigma and discrimination, and the consequences of exclusionary policymaking, some governments have established employment goals with associated financial penalties. My learned experience indicates these do not work, with employers willing to pay the penalties and consider that expense a normal cost of business, and still not hire any persons with disabilities.

In some cases, employers may find themselves at a loss for where to begin because they lack context about the contributions that persons with disabilities can provide to their industries. These outcomes lead to political costs for those who create and enforce regulations, especially when the results fall short of intended targets.

Economic Costs of Exclusion.

The American Institutes of Research (AIR) in Washington, DC, is a leading research entity/think tank that has excellent data on the economic costs of disability and exclusion. I quote it herein to bolster the case on the economic costs of Disability Inclusion.

According to AIR, people with disabilities have tremendous upside potential to be an even more impactful market force if we are able to secure employment and use a growing amount of discretionary income to be a collective economic community force. Conversely, continuing to deny our participation through discrimination and a lack of inclusivity restricts the amount of discretionary income we can obtain and contribute to the economy as a whole. This is an extraordinary loss simply due to disability exclusion from the workforce and thus the marketplace.

Estimates suggest that nations forego up to 7% of their Gross Domestic Product (GDP) due to the exclusion of persons with disabilities (United Nations Division for Social Policy and Development n.d.). Contributing factors for this estimate include the interplay between low investment in accessible education, leading to un- and underemployment, which increases the likelihood of poverty and dependence on social welfare programs (Kanady, Muncie, and Missimer 2020; Banks and Polack 2015). Such outcomes are perpetuated when public policies are created that do not consider the unique experience of persons with disabilities. As a result of exclusion, countries are not able to tap into the full potential of their citizens to realize the benefits of their contributions. We see this play out directly at the company level.

When employers fail to see persons with disabilities as both contributors and consumers, they squander opportunities to expand market share and create economic and social value. Reinforcing how distasteful I find this practice, the need to establish a "business case" for Disability Inclusion has continued to be a convenient reason for employers to avoid addressing their recruitment, hiring, and retention strategies. In the twenty-first century, this excuse rings hollow. Regarding persons with disabilities as contributors, there is a wealth of information that clearly shows how inclusion makes perfect sense and benefits the business. Studies find that firms that make inclusion a priority are four times more likely to generate higher shareholder returns within their industries (Accenture 2018). A rolling survey conducted here in the United States shows that approximately 58% of workplace accommodations for persons with disabilities could be made at no cost, and the investment for other situations averaged to be just $500. More importantly, for this nominal cost, firms experienced higher levels of retention and productivity, along with greater workforce diversity and morale (Job Accommodation Network 2019).

It stands to reason that the inclusion of persons with disabilities as workplace contributors leads to a more significant opportunity to address their potential as consumers. Estimates suggest that persons with disabilities have a combined $1.2 trillion annual disposable income worldwide (Donovan 2016). In the United States alone, the population of people with disabilities has a collective disposable income of $490 billion. Despite these staggering figures, people with disabilities are largely ignored as a target market for employers, beyond niche products and services. Much of the private sector fails to recognize that persons with disabilities represent a major untapped market segment. One report suggests that employers can reach up to four times their target number of consumers if they design products and services that meet the needs of diverse groups (PwC Australia 2019). This is especially true for the information and communication technology (ICT) market, with near limitless levels of economic and social benefits. Yet, they have not been realized despite a noted trend of increased accessibility features for both new products and services (G3ict and Knowbility 2019). Runway of Dreams convinced Tommy Hilfiger's President and CEO Gary Shaheen that clothing designed for ease of use for people with disabilities and seniors would open new markets for the Hilfiger line—the adaptive clothing market is estimated to grow from $278.9 billion in 2017 to $400 billion by 2026 (Coherent Market Insights 2018; Gaffney 2019).

My Inside Out Theory: Most compelling is the opportunity to simultaneously capitalize on the contributor and consumer benefits offered by persons with disabilities. By directly employing persons with disabilities to inform the design of products and services, employers create an environment where individuals are addressing barriers for others with a shared experience. This leads to a virtuous cycle of value creation for all stakeholders. Despite the clear case for inclusion, persons with disabilities still face unemployment levels that average double the rate of their nondisabled peers in developed countries and upwards of 80% in other parts of the world (United Nations Division for Social Policy and Development n.d.).

***

As a group, persons with disabilities are less likely to experience economic, geographic, and social mobility. As a result, how much opportunity is forgone within industries, nations, and across the world due to this unfulfilled potential? The growing demand for skilled workers, addressed through investment in education and workforce development, is apparent. Persons with disabilities, however, are not often associated with the label of "skilled" workers due to persistent discrimination.

3 Disability Is Essential to the Diversity, Equity, and Inclusion (DEI) Movement

When we talk about diversity, equity, and inclusion (DEI), what do we mean? Yes, we want safe, welcoming workspaces that provide opportunities for everyone, but it's more nuanced than that. DEI reminds us how to proceed when handling human interactions in the workplace, particularly those that impact a person's feelings of safety, respect, and participation. It is more than a catchall, the three pieces of the DEI puzzle are not interchangeable.

Typically, companies market this movement as a crucial trifecta, and sometimes they explain it as one conglomerate concept. Each word interweaves beautifully with the other two, and I think it's equally important to recognize the value in the individual components that build the whole.

For this reason, I begin this section on DEI by examining a theory of how the DEI movement possibly began, and then reviewing how we define these words in work and political settings. From there, I will backtrack through some disability studies theory and continue to examine how disability studies and a disability lived experience provide unique contributions to the DEI movement.

Where the DEI Movement May Have Originated

DEI may have originated with parents fighting for their children with disabilities to be included in local public schools, according to Dr. Jim Rimmer, the inaugural Lakeshore Foundation Endowed Chair in Health Promotion and Rehabilitation Sciences and director of the Lakeshore Foundation/UAB Collaborative.

Before the mid-1970s, most children with disabilities were educated in "special" schools for "special" children. The word in itself was offensive to parents and children who didn't want to be labeled special; all they wanted was to be accepted. Sadly, children with disabilities would "graduate" from a school system void of the critical social contact with all of their so-called peers. Given the generally poor quality of early special education delivered in special schools, these students were significantly underprepared to enter college, let alone the workforce. Many returned home to live with their parents for much of their adult life.

Sally Field's performance in the movie *Forrest Gump* showed how challenging it was to get a "special" child into the local public school, having to offer a quid pro quo—i.e. a tryst—with an older, sleazy principal so that Forrest could be admitted into the school. Riva Lehrer's story in *Golem Girl*, about a woman with spina bifida who attended a segregated school in the 1960s, described her experience this way:

> Our bus was painted with CONDON SCHOOL in big block letters, so we were always 100% visible as we made the rounds. Certain blocks were best traveled with our heads ducked below the window line. The projectiles might be rocks, or water balloons, or eggs. The splattering of yellow yolks on a yellow bus leaves it

bubbled and swollen, a plague bus carrying an infectious cargo. If I was stupid enough to tell anyone where I went to school, they'd look puzzled and say, "But you don't seem . . . uh . . ." The R-word wasn't forbidden; strangers just didn't seem to know how to rate my "intelligence." (Lehrer, 2020)

Thankfully, in 1975 the federal government passed legislation requiring all children with disabilities the right to a free, appropriate public education, abbreviated as FAPE. This began the ending of segregation for students with disabilities generally. However, there has been a resurgence of desire among students with disabilities—and even more so by their parents—that they should attend and be educated only with other students with disabilities, believing in the new theories, such as personal decision making and "control and choices," which are deeply respected in Disability Culture.

The FAPE standard does not deny students with disabilities the right to be educated in disability-exclusive schools. For higher education, think HBCUs, Historically Black Colleges & Universities, which are embraced and revered more than at any time in the past 50 years. Given the strife that exists for belonging to any marginalized, minority group and the frightening uptick in the false promises of White Supremacy, anyone identifying with a minority group, including people with disabilities, finds comfort and mutual support from belonging to a group, a school, a social club where no one questions one's rightful belonging.

At the Henry Viscardi School (HVS) in Albertson, New York, where I served as President for nearly 11 years, only students with disabilities may attend. To refer a disabled student to HVS—a private, not-for-profit for preschool through 12th grade—the public school proceeds through a short series of interviews with parents of the students and the students themselves, if age appropriate, to ensure the reasons for the referral are warranted. Independently, parents of disabled students may petition the New York State Commissioner of Education for approval of the placement with HVS or another, similar "4201"school (how New York State classifies schools serving deaf, blind and physically disabled students). Incidentally, there is another set of schools for students with I/DD (intellectual and developmental disabilities): "853" schools, named after the New York State law which authorizes both sets of schools. Several years ago, less than one-half of New York City's public schools were accessible to students with mobility-related disabilities, and referral to HVS or another private school was easily approved. In this debate about placement, great deference was given to the choice requested by the student and their parents. My experience clearly told me HVS students were thriving because they had a fully accessible curriculum, a fully accessible school and all facilities, and there was never a neglected student who was overlooked and avoided by the outstanding teachers, therapists (related services professionals), and administrators due to complexities and misunderstandings about a student's disability.

Choice and control over one's life are mainstay theories and tenets of Disability Culture. Respecting a disabled student's wishes as to where and with whom they are educated is an acknowledgment of the thriving concept of Disability Culture. In the ebb and flow of "separateness" versus inclusion regarding people with disabilities of all ages, what disabled people want is of paramount value. And, when these students enter the workforce, and note I didn't state "if," they'll more than likely have developed the needed self-respect and self-worthiness that allows them to hold their heads high and be disability-confident to perform satisfactorily or better!

The "separate but equal" theory was no longer acceptable.

The Education of All Handicapped Children's Act of 1975 (P.L. 94-142) built the backbone of integration for children with disabilities. Unfortunately, as with most pieces of legislation, it didn't go far enough. Early reports described children with disabilities being mainstreamed into public schools, but all that meant was that they were under the same roof with other children from the neighborhood.

Mainstreaming seemed to solve one problem but created another. Children were still being excluded. But this time parents weren't going to wait another 50 years for things to change. They, not the school district, decided what was best for their child, and they demanded that their children be included in the same classrooms, programs, gym classes, after-school activities, overnight trips, visits to museums, etc., as any other student in that school.

As we continue to expand Diversity, Equity, and Inclusion in higher ed, let's not forget the generation of parents who wrote the "playbook" of inclusion in elementary and secondary education 50 years ago. To me, the Disability Rights Movement received its initial liftoff with the power and advocacy of parents of children with disabilities more than 50 years ago. Before then, we should realize the Society for Crippled Children—Easterseals, as it's now known, and with whom I've had a lifelong relationship—began in 1917 when Dr. Edgar Allen learned that children injured in a streetcar accident might be left unserved medically because their families lacked the financial means to cover their medical bills. He started locally in Ohio and the organization expanded into the nationwide charity that survives well to this day. It was purely a charitable purpose for which he began Easterseals.

From the older medical model of disability in the early to middle 1900s, the prevailing thought then was disabled people must be "fixed" and "cured." With the passage of Medicare and Medicaid in the 1960s to serve poor people, and included poor people with disabilities, up through today, public policies began to look at today's understanding of the social model of disability which shifted, most appropriately, the notion that "disability that needed to be fixed or cured" to identifying the real barriers to our full societal participation, such as the built environment, the virtual environment, and nondisabled people's biases against people with disabilities. When this redefinition of responsibility for barriers and biases occurred, it was empowering to people with disabilities who'd carried the additional burden of blame upon ourselves when it was others who had built and maintained inaccessible and unwelcoming environments who needed to accept this blame.

Today, thanks to breakthrough thinking by The Corporate Board, progressive disability advocates, and strong politicians, among many, we have reframed the role of a corporation and even society in general to focus on Diversity, Equity, and Inclusion under the ESG (environmental, social, and governance) banner of corporate responsibility. No companies do this better than Delta Air Lines, EY, Barclay's Bank, IBM, and JPMorgan Chase, to name only a few I admire greatly. Let's explore this more deeply, and begin by how Diversity, Equity, and Inclusion are defined.

Definitions

Diversity is the variety within humankind. It is not what makes people different from the hegemonic "standard," but rather how we resonate when we bring our multifaceted identities forward into a mix. We do not want to lump or label people into the "norm" or the "other," We want to acknowledge that difference exists within a group—people are not diverse; it is the collective that is diverse.

Equity and equality are not equivocal. Equality denotes treating everyone "the same." To be equitable, we must recognize that we need to meet people's different needs to maintain fairness. Equity is when we provide balanced access and opportunity for all. Equity fills the gaps in support where and how people need it.

Inclusion is a final step in the process. Inclusion demands that we give every person authoritative power in decision making and contemplate their input with care. Not only is everyone present and able to participate fully, but each person's voice matters in the development and outcome.

How Do We Incorporate Disability Studies into These DEI Definitions?

Let's unpack how we infuse disability into DEI.

Disability as Diversity

Not long ago, colleagues informed me that disability does not qualify as a form of diverse hiring at some places. While it counts in terms of identity diversity in the workspace, it doesn't count in diversity statistics when looking at applicants because, frankly, "diversity" is codified through a minimalist lens. Disability might not be what we classically recognize as diverse. After all, people view disability in medical terms (the passe "medical model") rather than as a culture. How can we claim to be open-minded and recognize something as an identity if: (a) we outright dismiss it in the hiring process (or overlook it when seeking employees), and (b) we only count it as diverse when we feel comfortable or when it's convenient to promote?

Disability lived experience is a wide-ranging spectrum and often a very individualized experience that combines physical, mental, emotional, and societal pressures. Disability is diverse, let alone diversity in a giant umbrella of marginalized identity. Furthermore, disability is one of the only identities that can be acquired by any person at any time. It intersects other identities, and often people will identify as having multiple marginalized identities (i.e. a person of color and disabled, gay and disabled, immigrant and disabled). It's essential to recognize how disability intersects and affects other cultural identities because people will have to navigate their lives and the world differently. It's not the same as having one marginalized identity.

Disability Equity

For one, disability requires an informed HR department because, colloquially, "expect the unexpected." Things will come up. People will have to be creative with their solutions. This is so true at Lakeshore Foundation where I serve as president and CEO, and our HR function is performed well, and we "expect the unexpected," daily.

The disability experience is not always steady. A disability experience can be episodic. Some days may be better than others. Sometimes elements of our workspace that once worked for us no longer do because of a change or fluctuation in our bodily or mental states. Organizations need to be flexible and willing to discuss access needs for disability equity to exist.

Second, to be equitable in terms of disability, employers must recognize disability as a culture. Equity goes beyond the physical. Organizations should acknowledge disabled people's contributions and encourage their work. Organizations must provide the emotional space for them to thrive and be motivated just as much as the physical space for people with disabilities to feel secure in their job.

Disability Inclusion

What does Disability Inclusion look like in the workplace? When we are sitting in on meetings, listen to us. Sometimes our opinions are not popular. Sometimes we will say what people are not used to hearing—or don't wish to hear. People widely misunderstand disability and do not necessarily recognize it as a culture. Sometimes we will have to call out when an idea has projected overt ableism. Sometimes we will have to point out when a policy fails to acknowledge the needs and nuances of people with disabilities. If all voices matter, then we, people with disabilities, must be included. What we say has just as much gravity as anyone else's statements. And when we do point out the need for inclusion, do not end it with, "We'll look into that." Make a conscious decision to act seriously on our decision if it's warranted. Make an effort to explore our concerns and spend time and money on solutions. I have spent a significant number of years in meetings where someone suggested something offensive about disability and told me I was being too sensitive or too harsh for voicing my criticism to higher pay grade officials. Or I was humored and my complaint was entertained publicly but dismissed shortly thereafter. Or they rolled their eyes. Or they tried to justify why their ableist idea "is just another opinion" and I should "keep an open mind." You cannot do this to your colleagues or employees and claim to respect their disability identity. It is disingenuous.

How Disability Rights Informs DEI

In many ways, we attribute the start of the Disability Rights Movement, as described at the beginning of the chapter, to parents of children with disabilities at a time that coincided with the earlier days of the Civil Rights Movement and the push for equity in public spaces. Culture began to expand the definition of "all men are created equal," as the Declaration of Independence enshrined (National Archives 1776). We can trace the origins of the Disability Rights Movement to several pivotal people, places, moments, and federal lawsuits challenging the constitutionality of forced segregated education. Employers should include theories from Disability Studies in higher education to inform business practices. Cristy Oslund profoundly says in the chapter on the "Potential Impact of Intentional Interaction and Coalition Forming" from her book *Disability Services and Disability Studies in Higher Education: History, Contexts, and Social Impacts,*

> What happens on campus—the discussions and ideas that are generated here—are both a reflection of what happens in the wider world and in turn impact social movement, thought, language, and behavior in the wider world. When a group of people gather for the express purpose of sharing knowledge it is logical that they are likely to be the source of new ways of seeing and responding to events surrounding them. (2014, pp. 95)

Colleges are spaces for open dialogue, pushing boundaries, and exploring new thoughts. For employers to be at the forefront of DEI, they should create safe spaces to communicate ideas. Disability history and disability studies are imbued with collaboration (Oslund 2014, pp. 95–103). Oslund states that reluctance to include people with disabilities in education is a mirror reflection of the larger societal values (2014, p. 95). Anna Mollow (2017) aptly summarizes in her chapter on "Disability Studies" from *A Companion to Critical and Cultural Theory* that disability history is lesser known than other social "vectors" (pp. 339–342). Disability rights began in the 1960s and 1970s, springboarding off the momentum of the US Civil Rights Movement and key US Supreme Court cases in Pennsylvania, PARC

v. Pennsylvania and Mills v. DC Board of Education, upholding the rights of children with disabilities to a "free appropriate public education."

Disability activists began to question the medical model popularized in earlier decades that blamed the body and its function that wouldn't fit into nondisabled persons' communities. Activists promoted the new "social model" of disability that places responsibility on society to be accessible (Mollow 2017, pp. 340–343). Ed Roberts was one of the earliest activists within the movement. When he became a student at the University of California at Berkeley in 1962, he was a person with quadriplegia and the first disabled student to reside at Cowell Hospital. He and a few classmates fought for access changes to the campus grounds during their studies in the 1960s. Sharing their experiences in the late 1960s, they noted how excluded they felt and hoped to create change through defiant, loud social action—they even named themselves the Rolling Quads. They grew into an activist coalition, became nationally recognized, and they were the fire that ignited the enactment of Section 504 of the Rehabilitation Act of 1973 five years later. Not long after, in 1977, disability activists, including Judy Heumann and an Ed Roberts colleague in co-leading the World Institute on Disability, organized a 26-day sit-in at the San Francisco offices of the Department of Health, Education, and Welfare in protest of Secretary Califano's failure to promulgate 504 regulations.

Almost a decade later, in 1988, students staged the successful Deaf President Now! protest at Gallaudet University when again, the university named another hearing president, repudiated the eminently qualified Dr. I. King Jordan, who shortly after the protests became Gallaudet's first deaf president in its 146-year history as an educational institution. Deaf President Now! in my opinion, was the spark that fired up the national Disability Rights Movement, and resulted in the US Congress and President George H. W. Bush to pass and sign into law the Americans with Disabilities Act (Danforth 2018, pp. 506–510; Mollow 2017, pp. 340–345). King Jordan is a dear friend of mine and, with his trademark humor and humility, quietly acknowledged his selection as Gallaudet's first deaf president as a major contributing factor leading to the ADA's passage.

The concerns brought on by students were shared and acknowledged by activists in many other social sectors. Similar considerations indeed apply to the workforce as in schools and living centers. We need to make conscious efforts to include and incorporate disability-focused practices by employers, governments, and organizations. Just as society informs its microcosms, the relationship is reciprocal. Let's make space for disability in our school and work spheres. The larger community will become more attuned to it, especially in acknowledging the complexity of multiple marginalized identities.

Why Disability Matters to DEI

The Disability Rights Movement is closely tied with other activist circles: feminism, queer studies, and the Civil Rights and Black Lives Matter movements. Progression is necessary for society to flourish. Disability is unique in that it combines physical, intellectual, and emotional inclusion. It requires places to respect both the body and mind and its variations. Employers and schools need to think critically about the architecture, ease of use, and function of physical and virtual space, to appease legal mandates for disability. However, Disability Culture also inspires creativity in technology, art, and more. Disability Culture encourages trying new things. It also demands that places stay modern, fresh, and prepared for the unexpected.

The Future of DEI Because of Disability Insight

Disability access relies on new technologies. Because of our personal experiences, people with disabilities are aware of services, technologies, and practices that simplify and enhance our lives. Companies that embrace Disability Inclusion will also likely be more ready to stay ahead in developing new technologies and strategies.

The lessons learned by being Disability Friendly transfer easily to addressing the needs of all employees. Employers should accommodate all employees by offering as much work customization as possible; acknowledging their different learning styles; and ultimately, creating a safer, more productive work environment that reduces workers compensation costs and allows employees more time for productive work. The lessons learned by being Disability Friendly transfer easily to address almost all the issues facing marginalized populations.

With the COVID-19 pandemic, people now know that many jobs can be performed online or far away. Disability activists have been touting this fact for years but have rarely had companies take heed. Because of their lack of foresight, companies lost months of productive work trying to learn how to use digital space and accessible technologies for all employees. Disability-informed employers were better prepared to handle a transition to remote work. Imagine a future of DEI and productivity if we include the knowledge of people with disabilities? It can only be better.

Inclusive Design

Enabling Work by All

As I've stated in other chapters, it may come naturally to use terms like *inclusion* and *access* interchangeably. While they stem from similar logic, they are not interchangeable. Inclusive design incorporates accessibility practices for use by everybody, recognizing that every subgroup matters. Access design caters specifically to people with disabilities. This design practice applies to architecture, digital/technological interfaces, and consumer goods alike.

Though the 1990 Americans with Disabilities Act insists that locations and services be designed accessibly, in many instances, you will see access design in the form of a retroactive correction. Something was built for "standard use" (nondisabled/ average user), and the designer adds an update to incorporate accessibility features or physical alternatives when patrons voice concern. Access design is often used in these scenarios to adjust for the missing elements—a curb cut, a ramp, closed captioning, audio description, a screen reader, alt text, etc. Of course, any of these elements should have been included in the initial design process. Still, more often than not, they are forgotten until someone needs them or considered when people with disabilities are expected to be a common user—hence the design theories used are specified for a disabled user and are more individualized.

Universal design, as I discussed in chapter 1, tackles inclusion through an umbrella tactic, encompassing design elements that will cover the most users possible but aren't reflective of individual needs. The purpose is to make a space, product, or service usable by all by including accessibility and user feedback in the process (National Disability Authority, Ireland, 2020). Good universal design should cover enough ground to create equality. Still, it relies on the assumption that "one size fits all," therefore, logically it could miss things that require ingenuity. In their article on the different design theories, Persson, Åhman, Yngling, and Gulliksen (2015) state that while it is popular to design for all, it cannot be implied that one solution suits all. And that is where inclusive design fits in this puzzle.

Inclusive design recognizes human diversity as the standard and tries to solve problems so that each individual's experiences are equitably enjoyable. This takes a different approach to the same goal as universal design. Accessibility and universality are principles of good inclusive user design; therefore, a good design team accounts for them and many other elements. Inclusive design incorporates multiple solutions, tailoring the experience for the user. The architect or product designer will acknowledge permanent and temporary scenarios where users need additional or alternative options to have the most enjoyable and practical user experience. Whereas universal design has a history in barrier-free and access design theory, inclusive design is still a developing philosophy. A newer definition recognizes that inclusive design should not have fixed criteria as it evolves for the population. Its ultimate goal is to provide equally beautiful and functional results for everyone to meet needs and expectations (Persson, Åhman, Yngling, and Gulliksen 2015).

User-Centered Design (UCD) and Design Thinking

With product design and mainly digital services, the user experience is everything. User-Centered Design (UCD) and design thinking are two approaches to solve problems before finalizing. A user-centered design framework begins with contextual research on who will the users be (spanning the widest range of human factors), what users want and need, and goes into conceptualization for a product or service, which is then developed, tested, and researched. As the title suggests, users play a pivotal role in each developmental step—their feedback is invaluable to success (Gilbert 2019). On the other hand, design thinking is focused on generating innovation through action. It relies on empathizing with users or potential users through interviews and ethnographic observation, evaluating the problem using their lens, then building a prototype or plan and testing it. It could be considered a subcategory of UCD (Gilbert 2019).

To go into UCD in further detail, we have User-Sensitive Inclusive Design (USID). With this method, people with disabilities are also factored into the equation. Not all solutions fit all people and so it's about managing the expectation of what services and products fit what users (Persson et al. 2015).

Benefits of Applying These Inclusive Design Practices to Work

When we think about corporate culture, we need to remember that employees are as much of an investment as our business processes; purchased or created technologies; land, building, and equipment; as well as the client. From a purely financial and marketing perspective, let's assume you are willing to put the money, time, and research into designing and providing a service or product that retains loyal consumers. You want to know that what you deliver to consumers will be cost-effective, practical, and profitable. If you do it well, it will be! To achieve that success, you need a productive and informed workforce. If you're willing to invest in an idea, why would you forget to support the workers and their workspaces that can deliver it? Failing to make an inclusive workspace means you fail to provide the best service or product—quality comes from the top down. People will notice. The gaps will be present in your final product, marketing, and public image. That's just a harsh reality. Maybe you do well enough without inclusive production, but you'll miss an entire market. Tapping that market only begins when your workplace includes those perspectives and allows full participation. And just as a reminder, that market? It's approximately 20% of the population. Imagine being happy with only being marketable to 80% of potential consumers? Imagine trying to deliver to that missing market but providing a mediocre product or service? That's what happens when you're missing a diversified workforce.

Enabling Work by All

The article "From Diversity to Inclusion to Equity: A Theory of Generative Interactions" in the *Journal of Business Ethics* states that short-term diversity training "activates bias, rather than impeding it" and that new theories are necessary for genuine and effective inclusion practices, particularly *generative interactions,* which are "social connections and understanding needed to facilitate equity at the organizational level" (Bernstein, Bulger, Salipante, and Weisinger 2019, pp. 396–397). The article emphasizes that organizations need to counteract the siloing and self-segregation of employees and foster cross-cultural interactions where employees can bond with each other and find healthy boundaries to explore belonging and individuation where everyone feels safe interacting willingly and skillfully (Bernstein et al. 2019, pp. 397–398). Enabling work by all presents a challenge only in the sense that it requires everyone to work collectively and be on the same page as to what everyone needs and is entitled to in order to excel in performing work.

***

Part I took us through the societal costs of overlooking people with disabilities, which are extraordinarily high when viewed in totality. The toll it takes on the dignity and self-respect of people with disabilities has been enormous. We looked at how the time for entrepreneurship has come for people with disabilities. Entrepreneurship should not be looked on as a default due to lack of employment opportunities, but as a real choice available to people with disabilities who have the requisite characteristics to be entrepreneurs. And, by always including disability in all matters DEI, we're assured that inclusive solutions will be made and they will realistically benefit larger numbers of people, not just those with disabilities. Remember the wise Daniel Pink who believes great design enhances and captivates the workers and their workspaces, and people with disabilities should always be included in all design considerations. You are ready to move on.

What People with Disabilities Want Everyone Else to Know

In Part II of *Disability Friendly*, you will receive insights on what I feel people with disabilities want everyone to know. When fear is taken out of the equation, on both ends, this allows for conversations and open minds to better understand each other. Here, I will focus on what nondisabled people should understand about people with disabilities, and what people with disabilities should understand about nondisabled people.

As individuals, we need to see how our common traits of kindness, understanding, resilience, adaptability, and self-respect will allow us to overcome ableism by recognizing our common humanity. In doing so, this will guide each of us in how to adapt to new ideas, hold important conversations, and broaden our perspectives.

It is essential for us to acknowledge and agree that issues of disability are and should always be framed properly within diversity. When we examine disability in the workplace, disclosure comfort and corporate culture must merge for there to be disability-friendly corporate policies and practices.

The culture of disability is exceptional. As I share my personal story, you will learn a little more about me and my experiences that have helped to shape my disability identity. Through these life experiences, I learned the essential piece of Disability Culture is inclusion and now, I share it with you.

5

Getting to Equal by Erasing Fear

Why is it sometimes hard to understand one another? Why do we stereotype? Why do we fear one another? Believe it or not, we do not typically stereotype because of hate. If you believe in adaptive categorization, a theory within social psychology, we stereotype to save time. Adaptive categorization is a method for people to analyze survival scenarios and understand those of other groups. "Stereotypes are closely linked to prejudices, emotion-centered judgments or evaluations about people based on their perceived membership in a particular group" (Heinzen and Goodfriend 2019, p. 270).

Adaptive categorization is, to some degree, a form of lazy evolution—intended only for quick threat evaluation (Heinzen and Goodfriend 2019, pp. 270–272). Furthermore, this adaptive behavior suggests we first align ourselves with closer ties and then the larger community for comfort, safety, and resources. It is time we recognize that we have emotionally moved beyond needing to do this in most daily situations. However, our instinct is to understand and emotionally bond with people of our chosen in-groups—those most like us—and to be curious or insecure around those of out-groups. To counteract this, we must take the time to understand those we designate as "out-groups." We will find things that bond us, and former assumptions or categorizations will start to mean less. Most of our perceived beliefs are emotion-based or non-rational, not fact-based, so we can use communication to clear up misunderstandings (Heinzen and Goodfriend 2019, pp.270–272). We can get to equality by erasing fear and clearing up misconceptions between those with and without disabilities.

People constantly make assumptions about what they think I can or cannot do, physically. I've been asked if I have other non-visible physical anomalies, by which I'm completely offended! You cannot imagine the absurdly ignorant questions or comments that I've heard, directly to my face or loud enough that I hear them. But what really offends me most are the times in which I am left alone when at a social gathering or a work-related conference, and people can't find it within themselves to connect with me. I have a very healthy view of myself, think I'm quite approachable, and know I bear at least 50% of the responsibility to meet people "where they are" and carry on socially. At times, I still feel I'm the outsider, am made to feel amazingly bad, offended, and put off. I also won't allow myself to be made to feel the object of sympathy so when circumstances arise like these, I exit. And that's why inclusion and being Disability Friendly must prevail!

So let's open up the conversation. Here are some prompts to get us thinking.

What Disabled People Want Nondisabled People to Know

1. "I am not your inspiration."

    People with disabilities want us to veer away from finding people with disabilities as "inspirational." Why is this a problem? Placing us on a pedestal of inspiration is a form of exoticism that undermines our capabilities and resilience to adapt while using our struggles to make nondisabled people feel motivated to work harder. Find healthy ways to motivate your drive from within yourself, not from the outside. Healthy validation comes from oneself, not others. Outsourcing is unhealthy as we create our own success.

As a person with a disability, carrying my groceries home should not inspire a waterfall of tears. I'm being facetious, of course, but it genuinely is not worthy of a gold star sticker. I may need to do it differently, using my arms instead of my hands because of a lack of grip strength, but it is not necessarily inspiring. I adapted, and it is no big deal for me. Today, we say loudly, "We are not your inspiration porn!"

Nor should my daily responsibilities as a person with a disability make you think that if I could do them, why didn't you do your daily tasks today? I'm doing a typical weekly task. I have no idea why you did not do whatever you set out to do. And frankly, I wish you well in doing your daily chores when it feels right for you. Be kind to yourself. We all have times when we just do not have the time or energy to do what we hope to do.

2. "Everybody has their strengths and weaknesses, but ours may be more noticeable."

This concern is a complicated one because it has the potential to dismiss invisible disability. Whether you notice or do not notice our disabilities, it does not make us all that different from nondisabled people.

Everyone had a favorite subject in high school, right? Or maybe you hated all of it, who knows. Regardless, there will be things in your life you face that you will find come naturally to you, some things that take work to get better doing, and other things you just will never be able to do. The same rule applies to people with disabilities. However, for people with disabilities, it may include working with physical limits, mental health concerns, or emotion management, depending on the kind of condition, impairment, or mental health situation of the individual.

Ingrained in our way of life is a challenge to our cultural norms, that asking for assistance is not a sign of weakness but simply my and many others' state of being. Many people without disabilities have tremendous resistance to asking for and receiving help or support. This is one hard lesson many of us with disabilities have to learn: our interaction in asking for help is simply a social contract. I respectfully request your assistance, and when given, I respectfully offer my sincere gratitude for what you did for me. Sometimes, when the person with a disability demands the assistance instead of respectfully requesting it, and thus gets none, they deserve that response! Other times, people of whom we requested assistance think we're so limited in our ability to do physical tasks that they infer a greater physical or intellectual disability exists to the extent we are unable to care or think for ourselves. People begin to own us! Why are newer wheelchairs built without handles on the back? Because wheelchair users got fed up with being pushed into places they didn't want to go!

Either way, please leave us in peace about it. We do not poke at you about your strengths and weaknesses. It's not polite to stare, gawk, balk, or intrude on our privacy.

3. The environment and people's attitudes toward us are more disabling than our personal characteristics.

As discussed in other areas of this book, the social model of disability, and variations stemming from it, is the prevailing theory regarding disability. In the social model of disability, impairment is a person's bodily experience. The term *disability* refers to the social oppression that comes from caste and social barriers, inaccessible physical and virtual spaces, and discriminatory policies and practices (Letšosa and Retief 2018).

If you provide us with avenues for success, our disabilities are irrelevant. We will still experience our bodies, but if we have access and rights, it removes the majority of daily complications we may face. Accessibility takes more work from designers, architects, legal advocates, political representatives, etc., to be mindful of causes that limit people with disabilities. Stairs are what's disabling my opportunity. I could live in a multistory building if it had elevators. I could work longer hours and be more productive if my office space had more advanced technology to assist me, reducing physical pain from my workday's manual labor elements.

4. "I just want to enjoy my coffee."

I understand your curiosity about my disability. I'm different. Science, biology, and psychology are pop culture relevant. I also recognize people naturally want to learn about new things. Those are all good things. It is a sign of care. It is a sign of emotional intelligence. It is a sign of a willingness to learn and grow. However, there are venues to learn about these things, and there are times when these curiosities are invasive. I have presented on panels. Sometimes I go to conferences to speak to people interested in disability studies. These are all great places to ask me about my disability. I am happy to explain what I have experienced and how I have adapted and what I need to be functionally free and to be my whole self.

That being said, we are all private people with our own personal life. As a good example of this, Matt Conlin, a friend offered this: "I had a memorable moment that made me feel stressed and uncomfortable when people unprompted asked me to explain my disability. It was on a cold winter morning before work. I was already running late because winter weather slows me down physically. I wake with physical pain. My muscles tighten, and I have trouble with joint pain. I was in the queue at Starbucks in a busy area. The line was forever long. I was in a rush to get my coffee and go. As I pick up my order, someone turns to me and asks me why my 'arm moves funny' and that they noticed it.

"While I must admit I appreciated the observance, I did not appreciate the inquiry's timing or wording. I was late for work, already exhausted, and in physical pain. I wanted to get to my desk and chug the happiness out of that beautiful peppermint mocha. That's where the communication breakdown occurred. I said shortly, 'I just want to enjoy my coffee.' I could see the person was taken aback by my rudeness and replied, 'I was only wondering. Sheesh. Snowflakes.' The sad thing is that variations of this conversation happen to me on multiple occasions."

With incidents like these, people shut down the opportunity for both people—the person with the disability and the person who made the comment—to find common ground. Sometimes it's not the right time or place, even if it's the right question. Please respect when and where people with disabilities decide to share with you their personal experiences. The truth of the matter is that we don't always have the time or energy to educate you. If you are curious, you can do your own research and confer with us in appropriate spaces like panels, conferences, and educational events. One ask is if we'd mind answering a few sincere questions about what they see as different. If we're not ready, please respect it.

And lastly, a short one:

5. Sometimes we don't want your help. Respect our space.

It's awesome that you want to be caring and kind. It's also often appreciated when we receive help for things that our disability impedes. However, if we decline an offer to help, don't insist. Often, we say no because we can handle it on our own or want the privacy to do things on our own. No, it is not that we are being stubborn. It is that we are self-sufficient and genuinely would rather handle the matter in our own way. Sometimes it is even to prevent you from accidentally hurting us physically or breaking our equipment, such as a walker, wheelchair, or assistive technology. Please respect that "no means no" and move on.

What Nondisabled People Want Disabled People to Know

1. "It's a learning curve. Please be patient. I'm not trying to offend you."

As a person with a disability, recognize that people experience a learning curve with handling disability-related matters. Everything new requires a certain degree of trial and error. I have concluded, over my lifetime, that children confront those of us with obvious disabilities and only have about seven questions that need answering for them to achieve acceptance of my differences. Adults, on the other hand, avoid us for as long as possible. And, when they can't avoid us any longer, they make small talk to bridge the social chasm. As they struggle, I try to put them at ease. I don't have to do that, but I choose to do that. Some younger adults with disabilities don't feel this is their responsibility. It may not be. But it is my responsibility to get them more comfortable with me so when they next meet a person with a disability, I hope they will see the person within, not just the disability.

2. "I don't know what to do, so bear with me."

When we are exposed to new things, we may feel insecure about handling them. My teachers, coworkers, and friends sometimes would say that they feel weird asking me about my disability or how they can assist me. Sometimes that fear of asking creates issues because it leads to unhelpful assumptions about how to help.

For those of us with disabilities, remember: we teach people how to treat us. Sometimes it's not appropriate to ask about a disability. Still, it is good if nondisabled people can find ways to become comfortable with a person's disability or needs. It is good to encourage people to be cognizant of others (don't patronize nondisabled people or be rudely instructive when doing this). People who are observant or aware of you will often follow your lead and find you approachable. If you need help, ask. Set your boundaries courteously. Be open to the idea that people will ask things at inappropriate times or phrase things inappropriately. When possible, address it politely, correct language patiently.

3. "How do you expect me to help you if you won't talk about it?"

Here's another real anecdote: As a person with a disability, I once upset an educator when I said that her question about my disability was inappropriate and invasive. She slammed her hands on her desk and exclaimed something to the degree of, "How do you expect me to help you if you won't talk about it?" I replied, equally as angered, "Who said I wanted your help?" and interpreted her question as arrogance. That was a communication no-no for both of us.

People want to be kind. People want to help. They won't know how to help unless we communicate our needs. The key is to find a bridge in the communication where we both feel safe having a meaningful conversation that is mutually beneficial and not perpetuating a divide.

We can find ways to understand one another. Communicating nonaggressively and courteously will reduce the tension surrounding complicated situations. In your talent search for qualified persons with disabilities, we want you to see our strengths, our capabilities, our wit and wisdom, and maybe some of the intangibles that draw people together and form successful teams. While some stories are painful for us to recount and even for you to read, the bigger point here is everybody has these types of stories of good and difficult conversations, where people's unintended (and sometimes, intended) words and actions can derail an otherwise successful journey to employment. Keep this in perspective and please learn from them. We're so much alike, yet we have different circumstances and backgrounds. We all want respect, trust, and appreciation for good hard work in the workplace. With your learning about what might be offensive to us and what pleases us, you'll see the similarities that we all share. I hope they are helpful to you on this journey!

6 Overcome Ableism by Recognizing Our Common Humanity

One common human trait is our potential for kindness. We try to live good lives and believe in community values for the most part. While we are each unique, we try to bond with other people and find ways to interrelate. A remarkable trait of humanity is our potential for kindness and ability to adapt as we experience new things.

In the field of social psychology, we have what's known as "pro-social behaviors." These are what we do to help others and to assist ourselves to "fit" into our culture. Pro-social behaviors have individual and group benefits ranging from evolutionary survivalism to altruism (Heinzen and Goodfriend 2019, pp. 304–308). When we express pro-social behavior, we recognize our actions benefit ourselves and others. These behaviors can help us feel good about ourselves on a personal level. They also help us fit into social norms and expectations and attain a good social status in our neighborhood, school, or work. We subconsciously rely on kinship and commonality when we evaluate who needs help. When we do this, we emphasize the hegemonic social norms, meaning that we consider how we help based on the disparity between ourselves and others.

Who is like me? Who is not like me? Who has more? Who has less? How do we assess those things? (Heinzen and Goodfriend 2019, pp. 304–312).

We may wonder how we relate to others, understand them, and help them. We practice *sympathy*, *empathy*, and *compassion* when we want to be good. These three emotional concepts are interrelated but are not interchangeable. Sympathy is an emotional response of concern for feelings that others experience. We can extrapolate or interpret a feeling through our lens and develop a camaraderie with an individual. Our estimate of the person's experience is not equivocal. Empathy is an additional level. Beyond recognizing another's emotions and having concern, we understand the individual's feelings with more acuity and objectivity. We can differentiate the meanings an individual attaches to their feelings from our own. We can also communicate this information back with accuracy and act on it with empathy. Compassion is a desire or drive to alleviate the pain or assuage feelings (Jeffrey 2016; Heinzen and Goodfriend 2019, pp. 304–312).

Sometimes we get along and understand each other's feelings very well. Sometimes we disagree. However, even in cases where we try our best to connect, we will have moments when we miss the mark. These scenarios can be especially fraught with conflict when they involve microaggressions. Ableism is a form of microaggression against people with disabilities where there is favoritism of "able-bodiedness" over disability, be it overt or covert. Each of the following sections explores a potential scenario with ableism. It is essential to recognize these or similar exchanges and be aware that when they happen, we have an opportunity to grow and use them as teachable moments. We only learn through giving things a try. Ideally, through some examples, we can overcome ableism by recognizing our common humanity.

"I'm Not Here to Make You Feel Better About Yourself"

If you went to grade school in the 1980s through the early aughts, you might be familiar with the colorful, feel-good posters decorating the hallways between classrooms. They featured enthusiastic youths with bright smiles and catchphrases like "We are one human race," "Love is blind," or "The only disability in life is a bad attitude." Although these posters were well intentioned and meant to be "inspirational," the authors assumed a few things:

1. That integration requires the erasure of identity and experience: race, ethnicity, gender, or disability.
2. Denial that the hegemonic norm still holds the most power, a fact that does not disappear because we say nice things.
      With disability, these posters hold another particular subtext:
3. That living with disability has no positive outcomes.

Now, you may be thinking, "What can be so offensive about the word 'inspire'? Is it so bad that I sympathize with the struggle?" According to Merriam-Webster (n.d.), the social definition of the word inspire is "to cause someone to have (a feeling or emotion)." The definition seems noninflammatory without context. A person without a disability may view the everyday life of a person with disability as extraordinary because of the additional effort it may take to perform tasks. In disability studies, we recognize this as "inspiration porn."

Society places a heavy emphasis on physical, mental, and emotional prowess. Capitalist culture, to some extent, relies on ability as a form of commodity. There is an underlying assumption that the more "able" a person is in the workforce, the more they are deemed valuable to the community. This is a result of the Industrial Revolution and the American "pull yourself up by your bootstraps" independent mentality. It has been subtly ingrained in the way we evaluate physical, emotional, and intellectual acuity. We were taught that disability is a hindrance or a burden to productivity, success, and happiness. More slowly but in a better way, we teach that this is not true.

Limited social exposure to disability can evoke any number of emotions. Three common responses to disability are guilt ("If this wheelchair user can wake up every day and go to work with a smile, why do I struggle?"); inspiration ("Wow. Look at how well they do despite having that disability."); or superiority/pity ("At least I don't have [insert medical condition]. Their life must be so hard."). Here's the hard truth: people with disabilities are not here to make you feel better about yourself or inspire you to work harder.

In her TED Talk, "I'm Not Your Inspiration, Thank You Very Much," Stella Young, an Australian advocate who passed away in 2014 after her TED Talk (2014) aptly said,

> Well, ladies and gentlemen, I'm afraid I'm going to disappoint you dramatically. I am not here to inspire you. I am here to tell you that we have been lied to about disability. Yeah, we've been sold the lie that disability is a Bad Thing, capital B, capital T. It's a bad thing, and to live with a disability makes you exceptional. It's not a bad thing, and it doesn't make you exceptional.

Disability holds individual and communal value, and it can be recognized as an asset. It's time to retire phrases like, "Regardless of their disability . . ." and "Despite their disability . . ." People with disabilities have unique insight and knowledge because of their lived experience. This lived experience strengthens collective contributions to social spheres because it provides a different perspective on the world.

Disability does not make us bad or exceptional. If anything, it makes us equally human. People with disabilities want you to know that we are not here to become your comparison point. We wake up, and we go to school or work. We have families. We have hobbies, likes, and dislikes. We have talents, and we have struggles. There is nothing exceptional about any of those things. The only outlying element is that our bodies or minds may operate differently from yours. Because of this, at least in many countries, we are a protected class under the law. Ableism often leads to discriminatory practices, and by comparing us with our nondisabled peers, we are being asked to carry the weight of justifying our value. We bring our strengths, talents, and knowledge because we view the world differently. We aren't here to make people feel better or to feel guilty. We are here as equals and peers.

"Thank God Their Baby's Healthy"

This phrase is another example of subconscious ableism. Of course, we recognize that a baby's health is one of a parent's top concerns during pregnancy. Doctors give regular checkups, proper care, and recommendations. Family and friends also provide guidance and reassurance. If a disability is documented at any point during pre- or post-natal development, a natural reaction from the family may be, "How do we fix it?" or "Can it be cured?" Grief is a natural response when you're told that your health or the health of your child may be complicated because of disability or illness. People place hopes and dreams in children. They represent unlimited potential. So, why is it problematic when we idolize health and admonish disability? It has to do with the history of eugenics in the United States.

Sir Francis Galton coined the term *eugenics* in the late 1800s, defining it as a means to improve hereditary "stock" (Grenon and Merrick 2014). There's a long history of eugenics within the United States that encouraged and promoted the notion that life with disability is less valuable than nondisabled lives and problematic to the community's overall health (Grenon and Merrick 2014). Because of this history, medical practices were developed to assist parents in determining which births were worthy of coming to term and which were recommended for termination.

We, people with disabilities, want you to know that we can and do lead fulfilling, happy, successful, and productive lives. It is also important, however, to note that in the United States, patients have a right to informed consent. They are entitled to unbiased, clear, accurate, and easy-to-comprehend information about all medical options available when seeking care or treatment. This extends to information about disability care, the right-to-life movement, and information about support services (American Medical Association 2021). The practices that emerged from eugenics, such as prenatal diagnosis and noninvasive prenatal testing, could be used to help assist parents in preparing for a child with disability, rather than used as a judgment on the value of a life with disability (Cavaliere 2018).

For this reason, take a moment to think about how the statement, "Thank God their baby's healthy," could cause harm. This could potentially cause distress, sadness, or anger in work or social settings. It is hurtful for many reasons, such as, but not limited to, when the following people are present:

1. A parent who may be experiencing grief and coming to terms with their newborn's disability and the necessary care involved;
2. A parent who is experiencing difficulty caring for an older child with disability;

3. A parent of a child with disability who may be perfectly fine with the disability and even supports disability pride; or,
4. An adult with a disability.

In any of these cases, the subtext being communicated is that the life of a person with a disability is less happy or valuable than that of someone who is nondisabled.

When engaging in this conversation in the workplace, especially, it is most appropriate to congratulate the family on the birth and remain neutral. The "disability lived experience" is complicated, and like anything else in life, people will experience ups and downs. We should practice sympathy, empathy, and compassion toward people whose experiences we don't share and try to view each individual as precisely that: an individual.

"At Least Yours Isn't as Bad as _____"

Ah, the age-old "Who Has It Worse" game. We all know *that* person—the one who always has to top everyone else's story or has to undermine and dismiss everyone's experience. Nobody knows a happier moment or a sadder misery than the one who cannot be outdone. Don't be that person. Everyone's experiences, good or bad, are valid. Yes, valid. When it comes to pain, undermining an experience can be very hurtful. It also harms the cause of diversity, equity, and inclusion. One goal of DEI is to have more voices in the room, not silence them or dismiss them.

Disability manifests in many different ways, and it affects each person differently. Everyone is entitled to feel upset, frustrated, or ignored. People with disabilities face their own triumphs and challenges. It is nobody's business to determine who has it easier or harder. Studies of identity show the importance of validating feelings among peers because they support healthy cultural identification, confidence, and mental health.

Moreover, identity politics can be empowering or oppressive depending on the context and the message. We consciously and unconsciously adopt attitudes about ourselves and others through personal experience. This is a dichotomy of societal values and self-conceptualization. It impacts our well-being and sense of psychological continuity (Söderström 2013; Zhang and Haller 2013). Put more simply, when we invalidate someone's feelings or undermine their opinions, we are telling them that their voice matters less. In a workplace, this is not only passive-aggressive, but it also limits the creativity and problem-solving dialogue within a team of experts. The more varied the contributions, positive or negative, the more likely a mutually beneficial resolution will be found.

"I'm Not Going to Sit Here Being Uncomfortable and Watching Her Eat"

A great friend of mine, Kathy Martinez, now president and CEO of Disability Rights Advocates, recounted a horrific story about a cross-country flight she took seated in the first-class section. A road-tested travel warrior sat down next to her and didn't speak for a few minutes. Then, assuming she was also deaf, I guess, started questioning the flight attendant about finding him another first-class seat ". . . because, you know, she's . . ." Kathy could almost feel him gesturing toward her. Before takeoff, these elite travelers were offered a drink and a quick snack. Kathy took her drink and the snack, and that's when this guy lost it. He stood up, demanded to be moved, and said, "I'm not going to sit here being uncomfortable, and watching her trying to eat." Kathy remained cool and calm, but she was mortified that this passenger wasn't being reprimanded in some way. There were no other available seats, and for five hours, they sat in silence punctuated by some "harrumphing" by the guy. Upon landing, Kathy received no apology from the flight crew but the rude passenger was rewarded with a free bottle of wine for having to endure the trip with Kathy by his side.

This is a true story, I'm sorry to say, and now you know a little bit more of what some of us with disabilities must endure. Shame on the guy, and shame on the airline, too.

Being faced directly with another person's disability can trigger feelings of discomfort. This could result from a lack of exposure where we don't know how to react or how to address it—the proverbial "elephant in the room." Limited exposure to disability may leave us lacking experience with how to handle broaching the subject. There may be a fear of asking about it or knowing how to ask about it. Here are some helpful best practices when in doubt:

1. Remember that if you've met one person with a disability, you've only met **one** person with a disability. Individuals are not representative of the group.

2. Let the person with the disability self-identify. Some people like person-first language ("person with a disability"). Some people like identity-first language ("disabled person"). Others may use other terms. It is not your decision what is most respectful to the individual. It is ours.

3. Become familiar with appropriate times to ask questions. While, yes, there is the phrase "Nothing About Us Without Us," and the newer "Nothing Without Us," it is also essential to recognize that it is not solely the responsibility of the marginalized person to educate you. Do your research and confer with the disability community when

there is an appropriate opportunity to learn, such as a panel, classroom, or conference. Sometimes we are tired and want to get our morning coffee, not be your "Disability Siri." It is up to us when we want to share our experience with you. Having to be the educator on disability education wears us down, creating emotional labor, heavy mental lifting, when sometimes—and maybe it's many times—the questioner is overstepping in their inquiries. "We're done with educating the world today," we say to ourselves!

Best practices change over time, but these are a few solid ones for reference.

Sometimes discomfort can lead to direct conflict. For many, witnessing disability is a tangible reminder of our own mortality. It triggers aggression because we cannot escape the possibility that we can become disabled or more disabled at any point in the life cycle. We fear what we do not understand. While some disabilities are congenital, many are acquired due to illness, age, or incident. According to the CDC (2020), "2 in 5 adults age[d] 65 years and older have a disability."

If we find that the conflict cannot be resolved through respectful dialogue, it may be best to step away. Having a mediator present can help find a solution that works for both parties.

If we witness aggression in the workplace, it is best to follow the company's practices regarding workplace violence and follow the proper reporting protocols. Human resources will determine how and when to intervene.

The takeaway is to practice sympathy, empathy, and compassion and to "think before you speak." If we can recognize ableism in social settings, we can minimize its damage. It takes practice to be an effective ally.

7 "You Don't Look Disabled"

Let's spend some time discussing the elephant in the room: visible and invisible disabilities.

If you look at most disability-related signage, it shows a stick figure using a wheelchair. Sometimes it will show a stick figure holding a hand to its head to represent deafness. The symbology necessary for pictorial cues is always based on physical disabilities because they are easier to understand. Because of that, however, people seem to forget that not all disabilities manifest physically, some manifest occasionally, and others do manifest physically, but in nonobvious ways.

People may say, "But you don't look disabled!" A response to that is, "Well, what does disability look like?" If you think about it logically, there is no clear answer. Most disabilities are non-apparent. And disability services are varied. Some people need mobility aids, and some do not. Some people need extended time, and some do not. Some need service or companion animals, and some do not. If someone has a disability, they are legally protected to receive civil rights protections and nondiscrimination in receipt of goods and services regardless of one's impression of its severity. And an even more subtle truth is that it is none of your business to know other people's life stories just as it's none of their business to know yours. It is a privilege when people share their truths with you, not a mandate.

In the Workplace: Disclosure Versus Passing

One contested element of disability access in the workplace is whether to disclose one's disability. Section 503 regulations promulgated by the US Department of Labor's Office of Federal Contract Compliance Programs (OFCCP) call upon federal contractors to provide numerous opportunities along the employment ribbon or path for individuals to disclose their disabilities. These federal regulations also set a target, an unenforceable goal—for disclosures—of 7% of a contractor's workforce having disclosed disabilities. Failure to achieve the 7% goal or target does not result in any consequence to a federal contractor, though failing to afford employees the opportunity to disclose their disabilities voluntarily does subject the federal contractor to potential liability. While most federal contractors do afford their employees the opportunity periodically throughout the year to disclose their disabilities, there's been minimal disclosures provided by employees with disabilities. Why?

People with disabilities don't trust that their employers will use their disability-disclosed information fairly and equitably. That disclosing a mental health disability, for example, could well jeopardize their job security and might end up in the employee's file that gets shared with future hiring managers. This information may well be non-job-related and should in no way be used to determine an applicant's or employee's job qualifications UNLESS the employer can prove the disability-disclosed information must be known to protect the safety and well-being of the disabled employee or other employees. That's a high burden of proof for employers to carry.

Bottom line: There's little trust that employers will use employees' disability-disclosed information in nondiscriminatory ways.

Academically, I have spoken about this in other chapters and other contexts. "Although employers publicly state commitment," Kuznetsova (2015) notes in their article on workplace inclusion, "it is apparently more difficult to change the priorities and preferences of human resource (HR) management and other employees" (p. 179). Furthermore, the corporate structure may influence the effectiveness of disability awareness and incentivize policymaking updates. Schein recognizes that corporate culture can be divided into three levels: "visible artifacts" (i.e. architecture, technology, dress codes, etc.); "espoused values" (i.e. ethics policies); and a third, less communicative level "shared tacit assumptions" (i.e. beliefs, perceptions, and employee feelings (Kuznetsova 2015; Schein 2017, Schein and Schein 2019). As Kuznetsova (2015) states, this structural analysis resembles that of Erving Goffman and his work on our presentation of self in our everyday lives. Some things are more obvious than others.

When it comes to disability, disclosure comfort relies heavily on how the awareness of a person's disability fits within a corporate culture on the three levels represented by Schein. I spoke about building accessibility and the use of assistive technology already in previous chapters. How do the other two levels affect disability in the workplace? How does a corporate ethics policy affect a disabled worker? How does a corporate communication structure affect a disabled worker? Do corporate policies recognize the importance of disability safety on a physical level? For example, how does the corporation provide appropriate safety guidelines and broadcast communications to people with disabilities? How do policies impact the emotional and mental health of the person with a disability? Do ethics policies include information on successfully navigating sick leave issues, disability disclosure and privacy laws, and general workplace guidance on appropriate disability language—the person-first versus identity-first debate? These are a lot of questions, and all have answers from an employer.

The more subtle question to unpack is corporate culture's "shared tacit assumptions" element. People believe what they believe. It is hard to get people to open up to a discussion about subjects that make them uncomfortable. In other chapters, I shared methods to start and encourage discussions about disability. Changing the trajectory of the "You don't look disabled" comment into a positive conversation helps to use the former two levels of organizational structure as a base from which to work. Companies with Disability-Friendly office layouts, the assumed use of assistive technologies, flexible work hours, remote working, and comfortable dress codes are already a step ahead of those without those guidelines. Furthermore, being ahead of the curve by updating ethics policies and workplace expectations documents will keep employees informed of standardized rules about cooperative efforts and general behavior expectations.

Even with policies, however, microaggressions are going to happen, but they can be reduced when the company uses visible practices and structural elements to support employees with disabilities. Visible disability discrimination manifests as people assume people with disabilities need help, whereas invisible disability manifests as the opposed response of "downplay[ing] the effects of disability on your life" (Kuznetsova 2015; Olkin, Hayward, Abbene, and VanHeel 2019; Schein 2017, 2019). Women, in particular, have expressed higher rates of concern over people not respecting their boundaries.

People with disabilities have the right to reject or refuse to allow anyone to touch their mobility equipment and/or bodies (Olkin, Hayward, Abbene, and VanHeel 2019). According to Olkin et al. (2019), in the workplace, women with invisible disabilities have "reported they are bothered by accommodations that draw attention to them," and several others worry over the anger, resentment, and jealousy of their right to reasonable accommodations.

Another significant concern for people with disabilities is how the fluctuation of symptoms, the episodic nature of some disabilities, is perceived. For example, some disabilities, like multiple sclerosis, have symptoms that come in waves (Olki et al. 2019). Also, when manifestations subside for a period of time, it is a misconception that this means the person has been cured, and sometimes leads colleagues to assume the person has been "faking" having a disability. Regardless of the current state of one's disability, intrusive questions are inappropriate.

One final issue caused by the dichotomy of visible-versus-invisible disabilities is that people without disabilities may expect praise for being helpful or, conversely, these same non-disabled people may even retaliate and demand an apology claiming the non-visible disabled people did not need help and misled them.

Disability needs are not usually explicit, and accommodation requests can vary based on an employee's current disability circumstance. Beyond training, it helps to have a disability-savvy HR department and generally flexible policies. A company can be forthright in its policies on requiring medical documentation that establishes proof of one's disability, if it's necessary to require such documentation at all. But, remember that the federal definition of disability is threefold. As the Americans with Disabilities Act specifies and the US

Department of Justice promulgated in rulemaking, a person with a disability is

1. a person who has a physical or mental impairment that substantially limits one or more major life activities;
2. a person who has a record of such an impairment, even if they do not currently have a disability; or
3. a person who does not have a disability but is wrongfully regarded as having a disability.

Even if you don't have a disability but are treated wrongfully as if you did, you have disability discrimination protections under the ADA. Saying to someone, "You don't look like you have a disability" or "You don't look disabled" may well allow such an aggrieved person, with or without a disability, the protections of disability nondiscrimination! While this "You don't look disabled" commentary offends me as to its rudeness and inap-propriateness, it stretches this issue well into a realm of social discourse that is beyond acceptable in so many ways. Yet, too many nondisabled people may feel exactly the same way ("You don't look disabled!"). My advice now is, "Stop and think before you say anything like this, and especially in the workplace!"

So How Do We Resolve This?

Clear and updated policies are a staple for respecting visible and invisible disabilities. One way to counteract these concerns is to implement policies that require disability education (for-merly known as "disability etiquette") seminars. Another, less demanding way to encourage awareness is to provide informa-tional packets that explain disability education and how to be respectful in the workplace.

And, if all else fails, it really is okay to remind people of the golden rule: MYOB: Mind Your Own Business. Really, at the end of the day, any peer-to-peer gossip about whether or not a person has a disability, whether or not they need or want help, is just *not the business of nondisabled people and it's only the business of a few employer representatives when justified.* There are public and private employer departments designated to handle matters regarding disability such as HR, an ADA/504 Accommodation Coordinator, DEI and/or D&I, and an Office of Disability Services.

How one looks or appears should be of little significance to others.

8 Personal Experiences That Shaped My Concepts of Disability Culture

Many individuals and cultures still regard disability as a weakness, maybe even an embarrassment, unfortunately. We've learned a great deal in the last 50 years about living with disabilities in the United States. "Fitting in" or "passing" with a disability often causes us to stop nurturing pride in our disability identity. Our personal desires to be accepted and liked too often overpower our need to respect and love ourselves with our disabilities, however different and wonderful they may be. Today, less than half of Americans with disabilities say that they share a common disability identity with other people with disabilities. Why?

Only 17% of us started our lives with our disabilities. Thus, to most people with disabilities, disability is a new identity that we have not worn before. Some of us age, or age further, into life with disabilities; others acquire their disabilities as a result of war, illness, injury, environmental degradation, or disease. Some of us do not and will not accept this new disability identity; I certainly do as it's the only identity I've known.

Born without arms ending just above the elbows and legs ending near the knees, I didn't know I was different until about age three, maybe four, when a young boy, very angry with me, said something hurtful. I went immediately to my dad for comfort and protection. For the first of many times, he told me that I was different—not better, worse, or special—than other children and that other children who couldn't accept me for using prostheses had problems, not me.

After Mom died, my dad's three sisters and his mother came to help. Dad left my two siblings and me with a sister for three months, taking this time to examine how his life had changed, why this tragedy would befall us, and what he would do going forward. None of us has ever known where he went, what he did, with whom he spoke, or what progress he made. He never looked back, other than to honor our Mom and to tell us what a kind, loving, and beautiful woman she was. Dad has never blamed her, or himself, for my disability.

My dad gave all of us children the gift of self-worth in being equal as well as different, in my case. Dad was our hero for his life of devotion to our family and faith, public service and advocacy, and his personal values and beliefs.

Dad began raising us as a single parent: Kathy, my older sister, was five, I was 15 months old, and Mary, the baby, was only three months old. He restarted his life—with two master's degrees, a deep faith, and without his partner. He committed then to a life of quality parenting, family and love, public service, and improving the lives of people with disabilities.

When he finally decided not to seek reelection to the City Council of Prairie Village, Kansas, in 2001, he had completed 62 consecutive years of public service—from a county road repairs worker, through a meteoric rise in the US Department of Transportation to being appointed Kansas Secretary of Transportation for 8 years in the 1980s followed by two 4-year elected terms on the Prairie Village City Council!

He spoke to us kids often about the importance of service to our fellow citizens, and he expected each of us to serve our fellow citizens who were in need. Both of my sisters became nurses, and I've been deeply involved in the nonprofit sector almost my entire life.

Dad was born and raised in northeast Montana where rugged independence and mutual support were the mainstays of life. He believed that to live in America, freedom needed protecting, so he served in the US Navy. His Catholic faith guided him through the most difficult times in his life. He remained an incredibly successful professional and even better "Dad" until he passed away from complications of Parkinson's Disease in 2008. I still feel I didn't thank him adequately for the great life he gave me. Maybe every adult child feels the same way.

My father's wisdom, charm, and good fortune led him to find and marry our second mother, Joan, in 1970. While he had had only 7 years with our first Mother, Kathryn, he lived a long, wonderful life with Joan for 37 years before Joan passed away suddenly after a hard fall on black ice at the age of 75.

Growing up, I enjoyed inclusive school settings from kindergarten through Catholic high school in Frankfort, Kentucky, four years at Georgetown University, and my three years at Washburn University Law School. I went on to work in the Law Department at the nascent US Environmental Protection Agency in Kansas City as an enforcement attorney, in an inclusive setting, of course. Three years later, I began my career in disability rights and advocacy in 1977 with the then National Easter Seal Society. Each workplace and workforce was inclusive, though there were only a few people with disabilities in my midst!

My disability has given me both insight and perspective on human behavior. A simple social handshake with me, because

I wear prosthesis, has sent ordinary people into states of total confusion. I know I must guide people at these times.

Typically, cultural identity phenomena are transmitted down through the families, as lore and legend, and many times, through places of worship. Our Disability Culture is transmitted from each one of us to another, peer to peer, for the few of us who inherit their disabilities. Yet, parents and families can and do nurture our culture. When my Dad gave me pride in being a person with a disability, he was nurturing a culture of disability within me.

In his 1995 book *Emotional Intelligence: Why It Can Matter More Than IQ*, Daniel Goleman, PhD, describes a core of emotional competencies: controlling impulses, managing anger, and finding creative solutions to difficult social predicaments. Goleman suggests that only 20% of life's success is attributable to having a high IQ, leaving 80% of life's success attributable to our ability to rein in our emotions, manage our innermost feelings, handle relationships smoothly, and keep in perspective our anger, frustration, and hurt from others. Aristotle suggested that it is a rare skill to be angry in the right way, with the right person, at the right time, and in the right way!

I empathize with parents. From the beginning of pregnancy, you've prayed for and dreamed of "a healthy, happy, normal" baby. Your world flips over when your baby does not meet this standard. You might think, quite wrongly, it must be something you did or some genetic factor. Please be assured that it is not your fault. My Dad and Mom had similar concerns.

So, that's just a quick bit about my life, but much more important is how the world has depicted people with disabilities in such odd and harmful ways. My Dad could only manage what was before him and how my views of it were shaped; he could not change the depiction of people with disabilities in movies, TV shows, cartoons, and the media in general.

The sad fact is, only 3.1% of actors on TV (and we would assume other media, too) have a disability (GLAAD, 2019).

For many of us who have grown up living with disabilities, we've heard just about every silly, hurtful, ignorant, and mean comment hurled at us. As my Dad would caution, "They don't know you and they don't know any better. Give them time, and even your time, to get to know you. Like all other disabled people, you will have to change minds and viewpoints almost one person at a time." He was so smart and intuitive.

But then, we had no role models. Circus performers and media characterizations of people with disabilities usually depicted us as evil or depraved oddities. Believe me, I've been called "Captain Hook" numerous times in my life by young, unbridled kids, usually in supermarkets, with whom I took—or tried to take—the time to speak with them calmly and respectfully about what they were saying. There's Shakespeare's Richard III and many of James Bond's archenemies, most of whom had disabilities.

It's also not uncommon for the villain to have a mental illness, along with a particular tendency toward violent crime. One of the media's most notorious villains for instance, the Joker (most recently portrayed by Joaquin Phoenix in *Joker*), is said to have schizophrenia, and the all-too-often suggested link between schizophrenia and violence has been thoroughly debunked, according to SANE Australia (2016), an NGO that has studied and published reports that someone with schizophrenia is more likely to hurt themselves, or be hurt by others, than cause harm to another.

A second media stereotype about people with disabilities is "The Superhero," as depicted in *Marvel's Daredevil: Season 3* by Netflix, wherein the protagonist is blind yet possesses superpowers, extraordinary and heroic simply because of their disability.

A third media stereotype about people with disabilities is being "The Victim," as in *The Hunchback of Notre Dame*, a pitiful, helpless individual (accompanied by an endearing personality) simply because they have a disability. Think about John Merrick in *The Elephant Man* and Tiny Tim in Dickens's *A Christmas Carol*.

In media, we are all too often the butt of jokes, one of which caused "the Slap" by Will Smith, an unjustified response to a comedian Chris Rock's reference to Jada Pinkett Smith's alopecia, comparing her to Demi Moore's shaved head character in the movie *G.I. Jane*. As Bill Maher, in his HBO show on April 8, 2022, editorialized, "Who else but comedians should help us set the boundaries of tastelessness and tastefulness? Sure, some comedians go too far, and we and they recognize it by the feedback." Personally, I thought it was a bit funny and could have been received as slightly hurtful, though not so terribly to justify an allegedly criminal assault and battery.

Other similar media characters include Warren in *There's Something About Mary* and Ken's stuttering in *A Fish Named Wanda*, all mocking people's differences to get cheap laughs.

Finally, we are depicted as eternally innocent, as in *Forrest Gump, I Am Sam,* and *Rain Man*, i.e. childlike, angelic, naïve, with a sweet character AND a disability, reinforcing patronizing perceptions that simply are not true.

I raise these examples because our Disability Culture rails against them vehemently, as these create wrongful perceptions and assumptions that must be corrected in the right way at some point in people's lives. If never corrected, these wrong ideas lead hiring supervisors to mistakenly apply these notions and refuse to give otherwise qualified individuals with disabilities a fair and equitable opportunity to work in competitive employment.

What Is Disability Culture?

It is not simply the shared experience of oppression. The elements of our culture include our emerging art and humor, our piecing together of our disability history, our evolving language and symbols, our remarkably unified worldview, beliefs, and values, and our strategies for surviving and thriving. The most compelling evidence of a Disability Culture is the vitality and universality of these elements despite generations of crushing poverty, social isolation, a lack of adequate education at all levels, silencing, and imposed mobility.

I note there is Deaf Culture which is somewhat different than Disability Culture in that it developed its own language (American Sign Language [ASL] in the United States and sign languages specific to other countries' languages) and was well framed before Disability Culture was defined so aptly by Dr. Carol Gill at the University of Illinois at Chicago, Steve Brown at the Institute on Disability Culture in Las Cruces, New Mexico, and Paul Longmore at the University of San Francisco (now deceased). While a good body of writings about Disability Culture has developed over the past 40 years, these authors are my three best choices from whom you could learn so much more.

What Are the Core Values of a Disability Culture?

- A heightened acceptance of human differences, whether they be differences in race, gender, nationality, and/ or ability.

Our lives as people living with disabilities have taught us to accept and be more tolerant of all people. Every day somebody tells me I'm different. Usually on airplanes, strangers sitting next to me ask three questions: "Where are you going? Where are you from? What happened to you?" Sometimes I want to ask, "What happened to you?" This question would cause them to think about "difference" as something that we all experience, with varying degrees of visibility.

- Disability humor, the ability to find humor in the strangest of places, the most awkward of moments, at almost any time.

So, I'll share two of my favorite stories:

I stopped by a restroom for a two minute bio/relief break and while standing at the urinal, wearing my prosthetic arms (and legs, but that makes no difference to this story!), and as I'm unzipping (that's as racy as this story gets!) my pants, my clamp on my right arm falls completely off, which is nearly impossible to do since the clamp is literally snapped into place and there's a secondary connection, a pull cable that opens and closes my clamp that's attached to my shoulder harness over my shoulder. This had NEVER happened to me before, and at the time, I was 32 years old!

My clamp fell off, bounced on the floor under the stall wall next to me and hit a guy's foot! OMG! What do I say to this unsuspecting and shocked guy? I needed my right clamp to finish getting my zipper up, and I thought minutes and minutes were passing, as time disappeared. Finally, I said, "Excuse me, could you please give me a hand?!" There was a pause, a good chortle, and the fellow said, "Yea, sure, just give me a minute!" We had a good laugh, and I'm sure he told a thousand people about this encounter, just as I've told tens of thousands of people about it! Stuff happens, and we deal with it, and the power of humor, though it can never be self-deprecating, creates a wonderful bridge to understanding and enlightenment.

***

Another time, I'm sitting on a plane in the first row of coach (because I couldn't talk my way into first class!) on a cross-country flight. The flight attendants were occupying a mischievous six-year-old by asking him to collect trash in a bag from passengers. He came up from the back, saw my clamps, and started yelling, "Wow! Look at this guy!?" One more time for the cause, I'm saying to myself, right? Right! He proceeds to ask me five to seven questions, and of course, one being, "Where did you get those [my clamps]?" I said, "From the Big Guy up there," gesturing with my head to what I thought was the sky and Heaven. He looked at me for a few seconds, quite bewildered, and said, "The pilot?"! OK, thanks for playing, I'm thinking! I laugh every time I think of his beautiful, innocent question!

- Our ability to read other's attitudes and conflicts in order to sort out, fill in the gaps, and grasp the latent meaning in contradictory social messages.

As our children—and especially those with disabilities—grow and develop, we should be teaching them a set of core emotional competencies, such as impulse control, managing anger, and ways of finding creative solutions to difficult social predicaments. Like good child-rearing at home, the lessons imparted would be small but telling, delivered regularly and sustained over a period of years. This is exactly how emotional learning is ingrained; as experiences are repeated over and over, the brain itself reflects them as strengthened pathways, neural habits to apply in times of duress, frustration, and hurt. The outcome—our children, all of our children—should be that they become very decent human beings, which is more critical to our future than ever.

Disability Culture has been shaped, framed, and fine-tuned over the past 40 years. In almost every speech I've given over this time period, I reference Disability Culture because, to many people, it remains new and interesting and invaluable in learning why the stereotypes truly hinder our acceptance as mere equals with nondisabled people and why people with disabilities have solid justification for expecting and demanding equity and fairness in all aspects of life. We rightfully belong everywhere all people congregate—in schools, churches/temples, in social arenas, in employment, on mountain trails and the high seas if we choose (and the accessibility has been created and continually evolves based on the new technologies of today and tomorrow).

We are not a bunch of angry, hateful disabled people who should be satisfied with what we've received! Hardly. We ask, "Who keeps building these steps with concrete and fails to provide us with equal access?"; "Why can't we find a safe and secure way to vote that doesn't unfairly penalize those of us who have great difficulty getting to and voting in physical locations and booths?"; "When will IT developers build into new software and hardware the universal access and design that benefits not only people with disabilities but also those whose preferences are for choosing big typefaces, voice-to-text and text-to-voice outputs, and live captioning?" These features should be as automatic as we once expected to get a dial tone when we picked up an old telephone handset. This era of DIY, "Do It Yourself," is difficult for many of us people with disabilities, because, for cost-savings reasons, businesses, governments, and educational institutions have shifted the work of pumping gas, buying airline tickets at a counter from a live agent, and getting cash from a bank teller to self-service options, on demand and available all the time.

I can't use many kiosks with credit card slots to swipe, so I don't have your choices and I want them, too. Developers must consider equivalent access always—and in all ways—to achieve the goals of full, Disability-Friendly Inclusion and implement a Culture of Disability successfully. We have far to go and together, we will get there.

My disability identity was shaped so well by my dad, two sisters, my magnificent wife, Sam, and from growing up in inclusive school and work settings. We are all products of our childhood and parenting, and most of the time, everything works out well, and in a few, they don't. I know how fortunate I was and am.

Inclusion works. Let's talk about how.

How to Become Disability Friendly: The Pillars of Disability Inclusion

Now that we have laid the groundwork for understand Disability Inclusion in Part III I share the pillars of Disability Inclusion. I examine how corporate culture, Disability Culture, and the DEI movement can best work together to ensure the inclusion of people with disabilities through the recruitment, hiring, accommodation, and retention aspects of disability employment. Done correctly, I believe these suggestions will lead to higher levels of employee engagement and loyalty across the spectrum.

I acknowledge there has been slow progress to Disability-Friendly Inclusion in the workplace and in the world. While our progress has been painfully slow, with this guidance you and all employers should see much greater and much faster inclusion of employees with disabilities in the workplace.

One of the biggest keys to success in this process is having the important and necessary conversations, adopting and communicating the appropriate organizational policies, and implementing proper disability-friendly practices. Your organization will be able to attract a larger pool of qualified talent with disabilities when your business processes are ready to welcome people with disabilities. Of course, that's a win for everyone!

By ensuring that physical and information and communication technology (ICT) accessibility are baked into your organization, you allow fuller participation and, we hope, success for you, your employees, and your business!

As a tool that I hope you find valuable and practical, I present a blueprint for the disability-friendly workplace of the future. I hope you use this to build, educate, and encourage your workforce and your communities to become inclusive to all people and especially people with disabilities.

9 Corporate Culture and Disability Culture

According to the Society of Human Resource Management's article, "Understanding and Developing Organizational Culture," corporate culture consists of shared beliefs and values established by leaders and then communicated and reinforced through various methods, ultimately shaping employee perceptions, behaviors, and understanding (SHRM, 2022). Organizational culture sets the context for everything an enterprise does. Because industries and situations vary significantly, there is not a one-size-fits-all culture template that meets the needs of all organizations and corporations.

A strong culture is a common denominator among the most successful companies. All have consensus at the top regarding cultural priorities, and those values focus not on individuals but on the organization and its goals. Leaders in successful companies live their cultures every day and go out of their way to communicate their cultural identities to employees as well as prospective new hires and their customers and suppliers. They are clear about their values and how those values define their organizations and determine how the organizations run.

Disability Culture

Disability Culture is what connects people with various disabilities across the globe, individuals whose life experiences shape a common, collective understanding of the condition of disability. This culture building is guided by an alternative set of values derived from the disability experience.

Despite general advancements on the technological, environmental, and legal fronts, perceptions of disability are in a state of flux globally. Those of us who live without a disability for years, and then acquire a disability, generally don't embrace the idea that they are joining this group of people who have disabilities and even embrace a culture of disability.

But there has been an emerging consciousness and discussion among people with disabilities who are increasingly vocal about their disability experience, expressing themselves through various artistic mediums. For example, every painting by my favorite artist, disabled Native American and disabled war veteran Ernie Pepion, depicts some aspect of his disability: in one he is riding a horse while still seated in his wheelchair and in another painting, he is looking out of a hospital or nursing home room from a hospital bed and there are bars across the windows, insinuating the prison-like setting that many people perceive in nursing homes. And the slam poetry of disabled people of color in which their lived experience now includes life using a wheelchair. These are powerful portrayals that educate and inform everyone through the arts! People with disabilities need to know that they are part of a bigger group globally, and that there are many reasons to be proud of who they are, both as individuals and as a group.

Identifying as having a disability is critical to this acceptance and ultimately pride in ourselves as people with disabilities. We **are** proud of our disability identity, accept it, and we talk about it because it is one of the ways we can get to the point of understanding and acceptance by nondisabled people in this world. By embracing it, we bolster our own self-worth and self-identity. We create cohesion among people with various types of disabilities, and we don't separate ourselves on the basis of having different disabilities.

For too long and for very good reasons, there have been parent-initiated organizations for people with specific disabilities such as cerebral palsy, blindness, deafness, and intellectual disabilities. Many of these organizations were started by parents to solve a problem or obtain services for their children, and they found other, similarly situated families. Today, we acknowledge there are common themes that run across all of us with our differing disabilities. That is what our Disability Culture is all about.

It starts with lifting ourselves up emotionally and psychologically—or simply starting at uplifted, to believe we rightfully belong everywhere in society. For too long we have been the apologists for being born with or acquiring a condition over which we have had little to no control. Historically, people with disabilities have been the objects of charity and pity, and millions and millions of dollars have been raised to "take care" of us, to allow us to live the barest of lives. Nondisabled people were told we needed to be cared for; they were not told the value or the rights we might have to live full lives.

We reject this notion completely. Today, by embracing our own Disability Culture, we are empowered and have gained resilience from and among ourselves. We don't mean we are "better" than anybody else, but we do mean we're equal to everyone else in every way. By loving who we are, just the way we are, we also have learned to respect other people's cultures as much as we respect our own. This is the greatest lesson for all people to learn.

Disability Culture is not simply a shared experience of oppression, whether the oppression was intended or resulting from ignorance. We usually ask: "Why didn't anyone think about the accessibility of a product, service, or a building? Why didn't they think to include us when these were being designed and built?" I think we may possibly have been initially, but to many designers and builders of our constructed environments, we were regarded as insignificant in our numbers (that's untrue as we are 20% of the population, and that's also because barriers kept many of us from living freely in our communities), too small to care about. And for heaven's sake, they never envisioned us growing up to be workers, supervisors, business owners, or consumers of goods and services.

Disability Culture encompasses our own strategies for surviving and thriving at a higher, more independent level. The core values of our Disability Culture are:

- A heightened acceptance of all human differences and accepting interdependence as part of our lives, always striving for economic and personal independence. Yes, we disabled people sometimes do need help with daily tasks, such as getting dressed or opening a door, but so do nondisabled people. We view our obligation to help other people in the way that we can as essential to our social contract with others as equal citizens. Many people with disabilities don't think that this is the underlying intersocial dynamic at play here with the nondisabled population, but it is. We are all connected in and through life. Knowing and understanding this is a critical part of our lives: We wish to live with equality and dignity alongside all other members of society. This is our Disability Culture.

- An extraordinary ability to tolerate a lack of resolution in our lives. Nothing's ever quite done or finished, and we have learned to live with that. Nondisabled people think this is the way they've learned to live their lives, too. Yes, they have! But we have had to tolerate what some of us believe to be absurdly repetitive requests for documentation; as one example only, showing that we really have a disability. Maybe technology will resolve this someday, but given the elevated frequency that some of us visit medical professionals, we constantly have to produce the required documentation proving we meet the eligibility requirements to receive the services we're seeking. For example, I have to produce medical certification that I live without arms below the elbows and legs below the knees to obtain a disability parking placard EACH YEAR, in some jurisdictions in which I have lived. I recall applying for a disability parking placard in Washington, DC, and producing the requisite doctor's signed certificate of my having my disability and was told the placard was good for one year, and I'd have to come back in a year's time to reapply for another one-year placard. So, I asked the DMV representative, "Do you think I'm like a starfish and I'll regenerate arms and legs within that year?!" I was frustrated and slightly out of line I'll admit, but given these permanent disabilities with which I live, couldn't someone have thought to suggest there are people with permanent disabilities who should get disability parking placards for two years, five years, and even ten years, while others with temporary disabilities should be given shorter-term disability parking placards. People with disabilities have to deal with these additional requirements (absurdities) that are rarely imposed as frequently upon nondisabled people. I understand governments must try to prevent fraud and abuse by policy but who are the defrauders and abusers of these privileges? Nondisabled people! It's frustrating and resolvable in more Disability-Friendly ways!

- The ability to find something ridiculously silly, funny, or crazy that happens to us as we live with our disabilities and without it being self-deprecatory. Humor is a very powerful tool and can be a bridge to understanding each other. These are the fundamentals of Disability Culture.

Another real example of true corporate behavior and an odd micro-communication occurred when, at the age of 27, I was co-owner of a disability employment consulting firm advising corporations on how to implement Section 503 of the Rehabilitation Act of 1973. Section 503 imposes affirmative action duties upon federal contractors to hire and advance qualified people with disabilities in competitive employment. We did more than 1,000 one-, two-, and five-day training courses on all aspects of disability employment over a seven-year period. We were good, and we were in demand. My partner and I traveled across the country frequently. One day we were in San Francisco calling on a Fortune 500 company selling our training and consulting services. As we waited to meet with the company representative, my back was to the entry door, and when I turned around and reached out to shake hands with my prosthetic clamp, it startled the guy so much that he jumped back and said out loud, "You just scared me. I thought you were pulling guns on me!" It took a while for him to compose himself, to stop being embarrassed after numerous apologies, and yes, we eventually did obtain consulting work with his company. But that wasn't the reason we did.

This does point out how micro-communications and being different in appearance can skew the beginnings of relationships, professional and personal. I felt bad for this fellow, and as we people with disabilities usually do, we spend time and energy making nondisabled people feel less awkward and embarrassed over their awkward initial interaction. While Disability Culture teaches us not to apologize for others' errors, unintentional or otherwise, I usually choose to make these "teachable moments" and win over the person, to get them to where they see me with my disability and appreciate and respect me personally. Then, we can move forward together.

To develop a meaningful Disability-Friendly organization, your employees need to be introduced to people with the various types of disabilities and provided education that is essential to learn and conduct themselves appropriately and confidently when meeting and working with people who are different from the nondisabled employees. Even a person with a disability cannot possibly understand all the nuances of the many types of disabilities people live with every day. Every workforce needs recurrent disability education or disability awareness training, so we continually enlighten ourselves to the variations of the human condition who will be represented or are represented in your workforce, your customer base, your suppliers, and your strategic partners. This work is never done; you can only continue to improve and broaden it.

What Is "Work" Today?

Work is now prevalently performed today without regard to time of day, geographic location, or the need to go through multiple reporting layers. Standards remain for time for completion, cost, quality, and quantity but almost everything else about work has changed. Remote workers are commonplace! Yet, for some individuals who have significant intellectual, physical, and/or communication disabilities, who cannot self-manage time, tasks, projects, and resources, providers/employers must integrate directly, or by contract, opportunities to work and earn according to their abilities. Our movement like no other is challenged to blend civil and human rights with competitiveness and innovation by people with extraordinarily divergent abilities and capabilities. And that's why we love the challenges of our work!

From meaningful work, people with disabilities gain self-worth, dignity, pride, a connectedness to our communities, our fellow citizens, our families, and our souls. We learn the social rules of harmony, symphony, and collaboration that inform our emotional intelligence and allow most of us to work with diverse characters. Yes, we earn money which is essential to our dire need for independence and self-worth, but more importantly, we teach our colleagues about difference and equality. Recently, I heard the famed jazz trumpeter Wynton Marsalis give a brilliant talk comparing jazz and democracy: how the drum leads, the piano follows, the base guides, and the horns float around and through the music of jazz; just as in a democracy, a few lead, most follow, some guide, and others just seem to float around the topic, the problem, the solution. Through work, people with disabilities learn to lead, follow, guide, and float!

Achieving a More Equitable, Embracing, Respecting World of Work for All People

Everyone must take personal responsibility for providing equal opportunities. This reminds me of the great US Department of Defense's Equal Opportunity Director Clay Haughton and his clever story about four people named Anybody, Everybody, Somebody, and Nobody:

"There was an important job to be done, and Everybody was sure that Somebody would do it. Anybody could have done it, but Nobody did. Somebody got angry about that because it was Everybody's job. Everybody thought Somebody would do it, but Nobody realized that Everybody would not do it. It ended up that Everybody blamed Somebody when Nobody did what Anybody could have done."

Don't we see this far too often? I think we all relate to this story about taking responsibility. It seems so difficult today for people to accept personal responsibility for something that they did or didn't do. Not YOU, of course!

Throw away all your stereotypes and assumptions; replace fear with openness. Treat us, people with disabilities, and each other with courtesy, awareness, and respect. Judge us fairly, but also give us a fair chance. Educate, hire, and promote us, whether we're children or adults. Simply treat us as you would any other human being because talent comes in all kinds of packages.

We all have work to do, and each of us must take personal responsibility for advancing the human rights of people with disabilities!

Attitudes and Stereotypes

Without a doubt, people with various disabilities—and I've witnessed this constantly throughout my life—have been subjected to unjustified biases and negative assumptions that have held us down, collectively and individually. Since I was a young adult and heard Dr. Beatrice Wright, renowned psychologist at the University of Kansas who studied nondisabled people's attitudes and perceptions toward and about people with disabilities, speak so brilliantly on this topic, I began assembling my views as to what nondisabled people thought about us and why. I've given more than 3,000 speeches and trainings and, in almost every instance, I raise my four theories and seek feedback from audience members with disabilities to refine them continually. Those theories are:

1. Theory of Spread Phenomenon
2. Theory of Generalization
3. Theory of Avoidance and Transference
4. Theory of Territorial Behavior

Let me summarize each.

Theory of Spread Phenomenon

Nondisabled people, when confronting people with disabilities, tend to assume that whatever disability or condition they can ascertain is far more limiting to us than it really is. Our limitations seem to expand greatly, with the assumption that we cannot physically or cognitively function anywhere near the level that they live with every day. Our "disabilities" spread across our bodies, minds, and emotions to the point where we are unequal to or beneath them in the societal hierarchy. We know this is happening because our lived experiences have taught us about the micro-communications toward us: their words chosen to speak with us or make comments to us. For example, "I'll bet you have a lot of trouble going to the bathroom" or "You probably can't drive a car." Or the shock they express when they learn I've graduated from Georgetown University, Washburn University School of Law, and have been admitted to the practice of law before four federal and two state courts.

My takeaway from these many encounters is that they can't fathom how I physically could have accomplished what I have, or that I couldn't possibly possess the requisite intellectual horsepower and determination to accomplish these professional feats already achieved by the 1.3 million lawyers in the United States today! How insulting it feels that they can so easily underestimate and dismiss me and others simply by viewing a physical, speech, or cognitive processing condition. They don't necessarily do this with intention to harm or insult; it's pure ignorance, I'm sorry to say. And, the solution is, as my dad would explain to public and Catholic school administrators and teachers, presence and proximity. "Johnny," as I was called, in the classroom was not only beneficial to me, as that's where every child belongs, but it was and is beneficial for the other students to realize there are in their community children with disabilities who are different from them in a few ways but are much more the same in almost all ways.

We must take this same approach to Disability Friendly, inclusive workplaces and all societal places. Our very presence and close proximity spark an understanding of who we are, and the ensuing awareness of our individual strengths and weaknesses breaks down artificial barriers, promoting inclusion for the long term. And we've given everyone adequate time by now to get to this acceptance phase. There are very few reasons that qualified people with disabilities shouldn't be in the everyday workforce. The more time all of us have in the presence and proximity of people with various disabilities, the better we will be at defeating the notion that one's disability does not "spread" to the entire person, and it need not eliminate anyone who is otherwise qualified to work. A disability is just a disability.

Theory of Generalization

It's so much easier for us all to categorize people, processes, policies, and programs than to address each person and issue individually. I agree generally with this, as my many years in Washington, DC, working on public policy at The Powers Firm or as CEO of United Cerebral Palsy Associations, Very Special Arts, USBLN (now Disability:In), ACCSES, and more, have taught me well that good policy includes the most people intended to be addressed with the fewest exceptions.

But when such generalization is applied to people with disabilities, as diverse a group as we can imagine, policy rules apply and so do individual determinations about eligibility for services or about possessing the requisite knowledge, skills, and abilities to perform a job or family of jobs safely, with reasonable accommodations to the limitations caused by their disabilities. Yes, I define this precisely lest there be any confusion with my intent here.

All people with complete blindness are not the same, do not function or process information the same, and need differing accommodations and supports to participate fully as business owners, employees, customers, vendors, and community members. Same for people with deafness or who are hard of hearing. Same for people with differing levels of spinal cord injuries, traumatic brain injuries, those who are on the autism spectrum, and so on.

The very best employers are those who assess every applicant's or employee's skills and the talents each has to offer, and maximizes each person's ability to use them well for the company's and their own good. Employers are human developers, and they have, under The Business Roundtable's Statement of Purpose of a Corporation, a responsibility to support and guide each employee to fulfill their potential if the employee wishes to do so.

Generalizing about disabled persons' abilities is flawed with dangerous and erroneous potentials, and it usually turns out badly for people with disabilities. Don't do this, and don't do it to your nondisabled people in your workforce either.

Theory of Avoidance and Transference

Here's the outcome of this theory, in brief: Children confront us; adults avoid us.

I love it when a child innocently and filled with curiosity steps close to me, usually in a supermarket as I'm riding in my three-wheel electric scooter. "Junior" says loudly, "Hey, this guy doesn't have any hands." And I say to myself, in my thought bubble that I pray doesn't break, "OK! One more educational moment for the cause." Because this is where understanding and even empathy begins, that almost all of us with visible disabilities know this is where change for the better starts. So I start explaining this to Junior and answering his seven questions, and Mom or Dad happens upon their son and they say, "My goodness, Junior is bothering this disabled man!" One of them grabs Junior's head, rotates it 180 degrees, and, sadly but not really, Junior becomes a child with quadriplegia! The parents start with the "No, no, no, no, don't be asking foolish questions and making this man feel bad!" So, we wonder who has the handicap and who has the disability among these three sets of people: Junior, Mom and/or Dad, or me!? I am doing fine. I have the disability. Mom and/or Dad have the "handicap," the preconceived idea of what we are all able or not able to do. And Junior is just being curious. Junior and I align; Mom and/or Dad only have to monitor the manner in which curiosity questions are presented; otherwise, let Junior ask which allows me to answer in age-appropriate, educational ways that allow Junior to see a bigger group of real people who have differences and live in their community.

But, adults without disabilities (I'm generalizing now!) have been avoiding us for a very long time. In another element of micro-communications, nondisabled adults only make eye contact from a far distance. As we walk and roll toward each other and pass each other, the nondisabled person begins whistling a silly or nervous unknown tune and looking up like there's a California condor flying just above our heads. There is no acknowledgment of my existence, as I am looking to see them looking at me. That doesn't happen! We—I—simply don't exist!

Here's one of our secrets: once we get three steps past the whistler, we turn around and we check them out, and we catch them turning around to check us out when they couldn't look at us before! So, I wave to them and yell, "Hey, how are you?" They are so embarrassed that I caught them with this avoidance. This is what some of our interactions are like. They just can't quite accept us as equals . . . yet.

Let's take this theory to the workplace. The whistler can't avoid me when we finally meet, if we actually ever meet in person. Assuming we do meet in person, they can't keep whistling and looking up and away from me. What happens? They begin to ask some questions that are intended to make small talk to "break the ice." These are mostly awkward and sometimes inappropriate. Our tendency is to put the nondisabled person (see, I assumed the interviewer is nondisabled, and I'll bet I'm right more often than I'm wrong!) at ease. What's permissible: job-related inquiries intended to elicit responses that amplify on a candidate's qualifications to perform the essential functions of the job in questions and whether any accommodations may be identified at this stage. That's it! No inquiries like, "Well, John, I see you're wearing prostheses. Tell me how you became disabled." No, no, no! I think you understand by now.

In essence, the nondisabled corporate hiring supervisor has now acquired my disability and cannot imagine how they could accomplish the essential job functions! This "transference" must not occur because their substituted and incorrect judgment will certainly ruin my employment opportunities with the company.

I must say when flying for work or pleasure, and my wife is not flying and thus sitting with me, the first three questions to me, with reciprocity from me equally, that come out of the travel warrior's mouth are: (1) Where are you headed?, (2) Where are you from?, and (3) I hope you don't mind me asking but, "What happened to you?!" Really! It's the only space in the world I've ever found where such disability inquiries arise so quickly! Why, I don't know. Possibly because we'll be sharing close quarters for a prolonged period of time so he—and I mean "he"—can get comfortable with the big unknown! Oh, you have no idea how many times I've wanted to ask, after answering question #3 politely and generally, "So, what happened to YOU (to think you can ask personal questions of me and make me feel differently from you)?" But, I don't. Do you see when I—the person with the disability and obvious difference—am asking the travel warrior "What happened to you?" it seems I'm the angry, maladjusted, disabled person who hasn't learned to live with his condition yet!

In social situations like a holiday party, where some people know me and about my disability as one of many characteristics I possess, and others don't, when nondisabled adults make small talk, they arrive quickly at "knowing someone like me who lost their arm in a corn-picker and has an artificial arm just like mine!" REALLY, I say to myself! I have met so many people who have said that, there must be 25 million one- or double-arm amputees in the USA alone!

In effect, they're trying hard to build a social bridge to and with me, so I don't fault their intent. I, too, have a responsibility in these social circumstances to anticipate and meet people in the middle, to keep people focused on why we're together like the holiday, mutual friendships, our favorite sports teams, the weather, etc.

It's important to remember that the transference of someone else's disability onto themselves will no doubt doom the employment opportunity for a qualified person with a disability unless this tendency is addressed directly and frequently through corporate counseling and trainings. We cannot generalize out of convenience about people and their disabilities. No one should be subjected to the possibility of substituted judgment about their job qualifications. Hiring decisions are highly individualized assessments, and that's precisely what the Americans with Disability Act expected when it was passed. No generalizing about people with disabilities' talent, please!

Theory of Territorial Behavior

By the mere existence of architectural and communication barriers, we relegate people with disabilities, who are adversely impacted by inaccessible buildings and inaccessible technologies, to a secondary role in the dominance hierarchy. We keep people dependent on others for help and information, for supports and systems. Think of a corporate cocktail party held in a place where there are three steps up to the social area. For those who can climb the three steps, that's nice but exclusionary; for those who can't, we must rely on finding a ramp or lift, or God forbid, being pulled or carried up these three steps. The disabled person's behavior is seriously affected. They are no longer peers, as the person with a mobility-related disability feels psychologically inferior and dependent and left out. There are very few of us who can keep our confidence up after we've been made to feel like second-class employees. This is the fault of the company that failed to hold a social gathering in an accessible place; it is not the fault of the employee with a mobility-related disability!

So, take away the ramps, take away this nice interpreter, take away the CART transcribers, take away the accessible IT, and you have a rapidly widening divide and people with disabilities languishing as second-class citizens and employees. That is not who we are as Americans nor who we are as inclusive, Disability-Friendly employers. We are better than this. We are here to make sure that there is never a divide, and that we are all together at the same time as often as possible.

What Does *Inclusive* Mean?

If people with any disability of any age can participate in any program or service, any employment opportunity for which they are qualified, any educational opportunity for which they meet the eligibility/entrance requirements, whether delivered by any governmental entity directly or using sub-entities/contractors, or by an entity covered by the Americans with Disabilities Act of 1990 or its ancillary law, the Americans with Disabilities Act Amendments Act of 2008, or more stringent laws, executive orders or regulations promulgated by the States and Territories of the United States, these programs and services are inclusive by law. To deny anyone the benefits of participation in any such program would be a prima facie violation of existing federal law. Only religious organizations and Native Americans claiming primary jurisdiction through sovereign tribal law can fail to meet these standards of inclusion.

What is most difficult for people to understand is that a program, service, or educational experience might need to be modified and delivered in a manner that is different from the manner in which the general public receives their benefits in order to make it equivalent to the benefits received by disabled people. Once this "different and equal" concept is understood by providers of programs, services, and educational opportunities, for people with a variety of differing disabilities, the degree to which anyone with any type of disability can be excluded will be significantly reduced and eventually eliminated.

Is separate or exclusive programming or service delivery ever acceptable under disability rights law? Yes! For example, you operate a community recreation program that includes a basketball program for young adults. A young adult wheelchair user asks to play in the league, on a team with no other mobility-limited player. Based on valid program requirements to participate in the basketball league, the community rec center determines that the wheelchair user fails to meet the minimum physical requirements needed to participate safely in this program. But it is now incumbent upon the community rec center to find or create a program that offers the same or very similar benefits of competitive play, exercise, teamwork, and other program benefits to the wheelchair user; this might include affirmatively identifying one or more alternate programs or even the creation of a wheelchair basketball team and even a league of wheelchair basketball teams. It is not currently necessary to allow a wheelchair user to play on a team of non-wheelchair users.

This has been the subject of numerous lawsuits trying to resolve whether an elite wheelchair athlete racing in track meets at the high school level should be allowed to compete on the same track in the same race as nondisabled runners. Overwhelmingly, federal courts have found in favor of disabled wheelchair racers as there was an effective way in which such racers could compete safely both for the disabled and nondisabled athletes at the same time.

The United States Olympic and Paralympic Committee, having merged two related organizations, has struggled with this issue of contemporaneous competition between disabled and nondisabled athletes for more than 20 years. The answer: For some competitions, where safety and fairness are assured, both disabled and nondisabled athletes may compete against each other.

Think of the remarkable and horrible life story of Oscar Pretorius of South Africa, who became known as the fast human runner using two prosthetic legs and "blades" for feet. His competitive times placed him in the top 10 qualifiers for the Olympics at 400 meters. He tried out and made the qualifying time to be a member of the South African Olympic Team in 2012. In the qualifying heats at the Olympic Games, he failed to advance, but became the first physically disabled Olympian ever to compete in any modern Olympic Games! Tragically, shortly thereafter, he was found guilty of murdering his beautiful girlfriend in a much-watched trial, and was initially sentenced leniently and then resentenced to a lengthy term in prison.

But, regarding his racing alongside nondisabled racers, the controversy raged on. There were numerous arguments raised that his blades gave him an unfair advantage over nondisabled runners. Studies were conducted and, generally, it was concluded that using blades did give him and other double-leg amputees using them an extra spring of distance that unfairly advantaged blade users.

The question usually comes down to whether a safe way for all to compete could be adopted, and where possible, it was allowed. For example, although her scores were never counted as if she were a nondisabled athlete, Tatyana McFadden competed in Maryland high school competitions and later in college at the famed University of Illinois, an accessible university since the 1950s.

Today, both methods of participation are allowed at the discretion of state governing bodies, and in every case, there are individual determinations made, as it should be.

The goal of inclusivity is to make each customer and staff member of your company, nonprofit, governmental agency, or educational institution feel accepted, comfortable, and able to share their ideas and thoughts without hesitation. Inclusion is more specifically the policies and procedures that an organization implements to integrate everyone in the workplace. Diversity focuses on creating a workforce with people of all backgrounds; inclusion is a measure of the culture you create that allows this diverse workforce to thrive.

"Brands must be wary of tokenism, stereotypical portrayals and cultural appropriation, which can come across as ignorant, patronizing and artificial, thus achieving the opposite of the desired outcome; in fact, these will often highlight the differences between groups, instead of fostering an atmosphere for a more inclusive and assimilated society," wrote Chioma Chizy Onwutalobi (2020), the founder and CEO of SCO Group, London, England, in her essay, "Beyond Buzzwords: Positive Steps Businesses Can Take to Promote Inclusivity."

Prioritize Diversity in Strategic Partnerships and with Employees and Act with Intent

Merely playing matador and waving a red cape in front of a group is paying lip service to a critical set of steps that corporations can take to advance Disability Inclusion. Employers must know what they're trying to accomplish and why. Thus, they must act with intentionality.

It's oftentimes easier for large companies to put resources behind diversity initiatives, accelerate hiring efforts, and invest in leadership programs or inclusive culture workshops than for smaller businesses with fewer resources who can strengthen their partnerships, including with vendors, and engage consciously with their employees through disability and broader diversity inclusivity programs.

We have learned—and many already knew—the first investment a small business owner should prioritize is in its people. To support a Diversity, Equity & Inclusion Committee, circulate disability-inclusive events calendars and newsletters and consider sponsoring events that are important to your employees and the foundation of inclusivity.

Look into creating employee resource groups or affinity groups, or implementing an inclusivity training study group. Start at the very foundation of your business and examine pay parity practices and diversity in leadership, which both may take time but are critical to long-term inclusivity. Committing to inclusivity is an ongoing process that won't happen overnight.

Prioritize Working with Diverse Partners and Employees

As Chioma Onwutalobi notes, it's easier for large companies to put resources behind diversity initiatives, ramp up hiring efforts, or invest in leadership programs or inclusive culture workshops. For small businesses with fewer resources, one way you can commit to being more inclusive is to look for opportunities where you can work with diverse business partners, vendors, and communities.

"For example, if you're the owner of a small business, your in-house team might include people who are very similar to you, but when you have the opportunity to work with contractors and freelancers, that could be a window for you to work with more diverse people and reach out to people from communities other than your own," said Onwutalobi (2020).

Lisa Vasquez-Fedrizzi, managing director at Cheer Partners, was quoted in a 2020 article, "Looking for Diversity? How to Build a More Inclusive Small Business," about the importance of the first investment a small business owner should make: in its people. "Reach out to industry leaders in their networks to see who can be brought in for a skill-up lunch-and-learn session to help drive the conversation and help create internal initiatives," Vasquez-Fedrizzi suggests (Heaslip 2020). "Create a DEI committee who can prepare a calendar of events, find newsletters you can share, research alumni associations and other places from which you can recruit talent. Sponsor social movements that are important to your employees and the foundation of inclusivity."

Participate in an Initiative

Another good option is to work with a campaign or initiative that empowers members of underrepresented communities.

"There is a new call for individuals and organizations to pledge to committing a percentage of their expenses to underrepresented communities; a percentage of shelf space for products from these communities; or a percentage of contracts given to talent from these communities," writes Onwutalobi (2020).

Build an Inclusive Culture

As a leader, business owner, and member of the community, inclusivity starts with you.

"Create a respectful environment and educate your leaders," says Vasquez-Fedrizzi. "When you build your committee for diversity and inclusion initiatives, be sure to remember that employee engagement problems among underrepresented employees should be brought forward to discuss, review and make organizational changes to address those issues.

"Everyone's voices should be heard—this is fundamental to create an inclusive culture. Support your employees in bringing their full selves to work. Walk the halls or having virtual coffee sessions with your employees—this will be key in knowing whether or not you are on the right path for an inclusive environment" (Heaslip 2020).

The importance of attending disability diversity workshops and training—as well as offering these resources to your team—cannot be overstated. Encouraging a workplace culture of inclusion is good for people, good for business, and good for society.

Diversity, Equity & Inclusion (Including Disability) Within Corporate Culture

Through Diversity, Equity and Inclusion (DEI) efforts, *which must include issues of disability*, employers can and should address corporate culture and ensure that equitable treatment among all employees and citizens exists. I recently was in a live audience listening to Rich Bielen, the great CEO of Protective (formerly Protective Life Insurance Company), address his priorities and the time he spent on these. Rich acknowledged that he spent approximately 40% of every day focused on the

ESG—environmental, social, and governance—concerns facing his company and being as certain as possible that he was leading his company to deliver on sustainability and equity in managing talent, and that, in governance, his board represented the various communities Protective touched through its insurance products. Forty percent of this CEO's time was being spent on ESG, including DEI! These issues are very important to your workforce, to retaining your workforce, and to advancing your workforce. Should any corporation delve into political issues, take a stand on Ukraine, hunger, pollution, human trafficking, and the like? In the past, most CEOs thought these were third rail issues—do not touch them! Today, employees choose to work for employers who dare to point out and rectify social wrongs, and thus, Rich Bielen focuses 40% of his time on ESG and that includes issues of disability!

I also greatly admire Ed Bastian, CEO of Delta Air Lines, who has taken strong stands about COVID prevention measures, human trafficking, and equity in talent acquisition and employment generally, and customer relations. While this has opened him up to a little criticism, there's overwhelming support for Ed Bastian—and Rich Bielen and the many other CEOs who are reflecting the new and expanded role that The Business Roundtable foresaw when it redefined the purpose of a public corporation, as follows:

Statement on the Purpose of a Corporation

Americans deserve an economy that allows each person to succeed through hard work and creativity and to lead a life of meaning and dignity. We believe the free-market system is the best means of generating good jobs, a strong and sustainable economy, innovation, a healthy environment and economic opportunity for all.

Businesses play a vital role in the economy by creating jobs, fostering innovation and providing essential goods and services. Businesses make and sell consumer products; manufacture equipment and vehicles; support the national defense; grow and produce food; provide health care; generate and deliver energy; and offer financial, communications and other services that underpin economic growth.

While each of our individual companies serves its own corporate purpose, we share a fundamental commitment to all of our stakeholders. We commit to:

- Delivering value to our customers. We will further the tradition of American companies leading the way in meeting or exceeding customer expectations.
- Investing in our employees. This starts with compensating them fairly and providing important benefits. It also includes supporting them through training and education that help develop new skills for a rapidly changing world. We foster diversity and inclusion, dignity and respect.
- Dealing fairly and ethically with our suppliers. We are dedicated to serving as good partners to

(*continued*)

the other companies, large and small, that help us meet our missions.

- Supporting the communities in which we work. We respect the people in our communities and protect the environment by embracing sustainable practices across our businesses.
- Generating long-term value for shareholders, who provide the capital that allows companies to invest, grow and innovate. We are committed to transparency and effective engagement with shareholders.

Each of our stakeholders is essential. We commit to deliver value to all of them, for the future success of our companies, our communities and our country.

Source: The Business Roundtable, August 2019. https://www.businessroundtable.org/business-roundtable-redefines-the-purpose-of-a-corporation-to-promote-an-economy-that-serves-all-americans

Culture is what distinguishes corporations and organizations from their competitors and brings honor to their workforces, customers, suppliers, and communities. The ESG movement has brought heightened attention to equity in employment. Creating and sustaining a Disability-Friendly workforce will be ever more critical to recruiting and retaining your very best talent. This can no longer be overlooked or dismissed if you hope to remain competitive in your industry and attractive to your workforce.

Talent Acquisition Through Outreach and Recruitment

For many years, the recruitment and hiring process at organizations has remained relatively static. Channels for recruitment, from job fairs, colleges, referrals from current or former employees, etc., lead to a process by which hiring managers, armed with what they believed were the characteristics to look for when selecting candidates, filter through résumés and screen calls to discover the "top" candidates. Of course, this process is riddled with bias, almost by design. Qualities such as eagerness, an outgoing and friendly personality, and so on, optimized to fit into the existing workplace culture, are prized. Those who relate to others differently, whether due to culture, race, socioeconomic status, gender identity, sexual orientation, or disability are often removed from consideration based on this prioritization of "fitting in." The new paradigm that must be considered is how can the workplace be structured so that qualified individuals fit in, rather than trying to recruit those who fit the mold? This should be a business imperative for every organization in a rapidly globalizing society where our collective values are that difference is good, and necessary.

Role of Technology in Hiring

One of the biggest shifts in hiring has been the exponential increase in the use of Artificial Intelligence (AI) screening and interviewing technologies to sort through candidates. From the organization's perspective, it helps human resources professionals filter through more qualified applicants, theoretically allowing for them to spend more time looking at the most qualified applicants and making a better hiring decision. AI is tempting as a seemingly neutral filter for chosen keywords or attributes, and it makes sense that an HR professional would believe they are only spending time on the best candidates that the algorithm has filtered out.

Artificial intelligence and other technologies used in hiring and retention of employees have undoubtedly changed the workplace. While there is much to appreciate, the speed at which these technologies have been implemented has not left room for employers to carefully consider their impact. This has given rise to discrimination and bias in organizations that is carried out via technology. It may be a flaw in the technology but ultimately it is the responsibility of the humans who manage it.

AI for hiring is still in its infancy, and the research to back up claims that recruitment AI efficiently streamlines such business processes and finds the best employees without discriminating simply does not yet exist. Such claims are made by for-profit companies with an interest in selling software, but different groups have raised serious ethical concerns about the metrics being used to filter for "quality" applicants. The UK's Institute for Ethical AI released a report in 2020 detailing how the use of AI for HR recruitment is not capable of "captur[ing] the complexity and heterogeneity of people with disabilities" (The Institute for Ethical AI 2020). Disability is not easily defined by any metrics related to physicality, emotionality, or behavior. Disabilities can present from birth or be acquired. Disability can affect how a person speaks, processes information, and moves through the world, or it can affect none of these things. There is so much variation among people with disabilities, which is part of why it is the most intersectional minority that exists. Disability brings along with it the beauty of unique perspectives based on the lived disability experience, and it has been shown over and over again that AI is not yet up to the task of accounting for that variation. Troubling as well is the impact that, by using AI and achieving a match or fit, an employer has included as many diverse candidates with disabilities as possible. In reality, using recruitment AI means that anyone deemed a match or a fit has only been compared to an employer's current workforce that has already been put through the AI screen, or that the employer is using its own estimates of minimum job skills or other characteristics believed to be predictors of job success. As very few people with disabilities will clear these AI screens or filters, using the employer's existing employee pool, with too few qualified people with disabilities in it, is inherently discriminatory on the basis of disability.

In fact, this is not just a disability issue. At a basic level, a 2019 study found that emotions cannot reliably be interpreted by analyzing facial movements. A scowl could indicate anger or disdain, or it could be an automatic response to a physical sensation. Facial expressions are highly dependent on culture, context, and personal characteristics, and current AI technology cannot account for these differences. The general progression of automation is to replace first mechanical, then analytical, intuitive, and empathy-based tasks, treading increasingly into what has up until this point been considered a uniquely human skill (Caner and Bhatti 2020). The mistake of many organizations is to categorize résumé sorting or an initial audio or video interview as an analytical task to be effectively managed by AI. In reality, recruiting and hiring are acts of intuition and empathy. They require understanding not only the hard skills of an applicant, but who they are as a person, what in their life has brought them to your organization, and how their unique makeup can bring an important perspective to your workforce.

Employers should be concerned that their corporate procurement policies and systems may allow for the purchase of technologies that can cause discrimination to occur. How forward-thinking was IBM in 1999 when it issued its famous corporate procurement mandate that called for accessible products and services? From IBM's website: "In 1999, IBM codified its corporate standards for product accessibility with the adoption of Corporate Instruction 162 (CI 162)" (IBM 2004/2006, p. 5). This instruction contained a mandate for the assessment of accessibility characteristics regarding all new products and called for the integration of accessibility requirements into IBM's development processes. In law, there is a maxim that says an entity cannot contract away its nondiscrimination requirements. Corporate, governmental, and other legal entities cannot purchase goods and services, including technology hardware and software, that causes discrimination to occur and not be accountable for any damages it causes. Every procurement officer and procuring entity should review its procurement requirements today to be assured it's not buying software that causes, or may cause, discrimination of any kind to occur.

Depending on your role, it may not be up to you if your company or organization has decided to employ the use of AI hiring tools to screen candidates. However, what can be adjusted is the accommodations process around these tools. If it is the case that the software is going to be utilized, develop a clear process for candidates to request an exemption to have a live discussion with a person and not to be stigmatized to their disadvantage by requesting the "exemption" accommodation. To be truly inclusive, this option could be offered to all candidates, but at the very least it is the responsibility of the organization to ensure that due to disability reasons, a candidate cannot be forced to interview in a mode that systematically discriminates against them.

Myth of the Average

At the core of the issue with AI is the notion that there is an average job candidate, that there are ideal characteristics that can be systematically identified and measured, and that they will show up in the same way for every candidate who is well qualified for the role. This "myth of the average" is pervasive in society, and has origins in the nineteenth century with the implementation of the bell curve by Adolphe Quetelet. He overlayed bell curves on many different facets of humanity, creating models of "physical, mental, behavioral, and moral categories of people" (McCue and Holmes 2018), and using these results to infer that there was in fact an "ideal" human. If this is ringing any alarm bells for sounding like eugenics, you're right. It was indeed a precursor to these horrifying principles espoused throughout the twentieth century. Today, eugenics is widely criticized and understood to be fundamentally flawed, yet the bell curve has persisted. The concept of the curve is that 80% of people fall in the center section, and that by designing any product, test, or service for this majority, it will optimally serve most people, and the other 20% who deviated further from average are such a small proportion as to be negligible. Of the 10% beyond either end of the bell curve, people with communication-related disabilities may well exist. Brilliant people who stutter, blind people who cannot direct their comments to a camera, people with cerebral palsy who will have speech difficulties, and others could all be wiped away from consideration. If they somehow come back around and through another entry way in the recruitment process and this alternate path back is known to the hiring supervisor, this still will likely be regarded as discriminatory.

An example that perfectly encapsulates this conundrum unfolded in the US Air Force in the middle of the twentieth century. Officials were concerned by a rising number of flying accidents, which peaked at 17 crashes in a single day. These were generally ascribed to "pilot error," but it became increasingly apparent something else was going on. The military turned their attention to the design of the cockpit, which had been originally developed in 1926 by measuring the dimensions of hundreds of male pilots, calculating an average, and building the cockpit to the specifications of that average. Wondering if pilots had simply had a drastic change in size in the following decades, the military set out to collect a new set of measurements. Researchers measured over 4,000 pilots on 10 dimensions of size and allowed for the middle 30% to be considered "average." To their great surprise, not a single pilot fell into the average in all areas. This led to the important conclusion that has become the basis of many arguments for universal design: If you are designing for the average, you are designing for no one.

This message resonates so deeply with the disability community because we are often considered to be "outside the norm," which can translate into "not worth considering." If stairs work for "average" consumers, students, or employees, that should be enough to get by. What experiences like the Air Force pilots teach us, however, is that sticking to the norm, to the average, in the end serves no one.

The lesson here is that when technologies are designed to be inclusive from the beginning, they account for natural variations in people and accommodate differences. This is what has given rise to an entire field called inclusive design, and it applies to products, services, technologies—anything that needs to be designed to serve a purpose for people. In an ideal world, technology should give us the tools to celebrate differences, and properly designed algorithms can give us the capability to appreciate the many facets of a candidate that would truly indicate how well they may perform in the role they are hoping to fill.

"Most Qualified" for the Role

Let's dig deeper on this idea of merit, which is often used to absolve employers of responsibility for ingrained biases in the hiring and recruitment process. Many hiring managers will insist they simply chose the "best" person for the role, based on their qualifications. In theory, this sounds fair.

Consider hypothetical Candidate A—this person went to a highly selective university, graduated with a 3.9 GPA, had impressive summer internships and volunteer experiences relevant to the job. Candidate B attended a local community college and then transferred to a four-year school, graduated with a 3.3 GPA, and worked at Best Buy throughout their time in college.

From these points alone, it may be easy to declare Candidate A more qualified for the job and pat oneself on the back for using these "unbiased" facts to choose who will be advanced for an interview. Perhaps a 3.5 GPA cutoff was set ahead of time, further cementing Candidate A as the preferred applicant.

But once you take a closer look at these qualifications, the structural inequities that come into play become very apparent.

Talent Recruitment

"Where can I find talent with disabilities?" Organizations have expressed concern that one of the greatest barriers they face to advancing Disability Inclusion is the inability to find qualified candidates with disabilities. The key is effective outreach and recruitment. To build effectively a talent pipeline of applicants with disabilities, your organization can develop relationships with a variety of recruitment sources. Such relationships can be formed through formal partnerships as well as meetings and ongoing contact regarding job openings and candidates. The investment will be well worth the effort. Not only will your organization secure access to talent that it otherwise may have overlooked, it will also benefit from other supports that can assist in integrating people with disabilities effectively into your workforce.

Recruitment Sources

Here are a set of recruitment sources to consider:

- Public resources, such as American Job Centers (AJCs), state vocational rehabilitation agencies and community rehabilitation programs, state employment agencies, employment networks (ENs) established under the Ticket to Work Program, Independent Living Centers (ILCs), the US Department of Labor's Veterans Employment and Training Service (VETS), and the US Department of Veterans Affairs' regional offices.
- Private resources, including those provided by Inclusively .com, which may include professional organizations,

consulting services, and companies with expertise in disability.

- Educational institutions, among them community colleges, universities, and other institutions of learning and/or training, including those that offer programs for individuals with specific disabilities. Most college campuses have designated Offices for Students with Disabilities, and these should be contacted for recruitment purposes in addition to career services.

- Internship and work experience programs, including those designed for students with disabilities, such as (but not limited to) the Workforce Recruitment Program for College Students with Disabilities (WRP), Career Opportunities for Students with Disabilities, (COSD), Career Gateway, Disability:IN Mentorship Exchange, The Viscardi Center's Emerging Leaders Program, and Project SEARCH.

- Nonprofit entities and social service agencies, including labor organizations, service providers operated by and for individuals with disabilities, and other such groups that may provide referrals as well as technical assistance on employment policies and practices, including making reasonable accommodations.

Peer networking, which can produce referrals from your own business networks and help you learn what strategies and partnerships other organizations used as talent sources. A local Disability:IN affiliate can connect you to a larger peer network.

There are various strategies you can employ to attract and recruit qualified individuals with disabilities. Some of those strategies include:

- Hold formal and informal briefing sessions (preferably on company premises) with representatives from recruiting sources. Integral components of briefings include company tours; explanations of current and future job openings and position descriptions; explanations of the organization's selection process; recruiting literature; a description of opportunities for formalizing arrangements for referrals of applicants to recruitment sources; and following up with sources and providing feedback on which applicants were interviewed and hired.

- Establish formal training (and deliver it to organization employees responsible for recruitment) on how and why to hire individuals with disabilities.
- Provide an accessible online application and use targeted recruitment and social networking sites so that job seekers with disabilities can learn about the organization and its hiring initiatives.
- Join employer networking groups that recognize and promote best practices in hiring, retention, and promoting individuals with disabilities.
- Post job announcements on accessible web-based job boards that specialize in identifying qualified individuals with disabilities, including veterans with disabilities; in disability-related publications; and with specific disability service organizations.
- Participate in career fairs targeting individuals with disabilities, including veterans with disabilities.
- Engage current employees or an employee resource group (ERG) or a business resource group (BRG) as referral sources and ask for referrals who would make good job candidates, and include employees with disabilities in organizational recruitment teams.
- Build talent sources of youth and young adults with disabilities who are transitioning high school and college

students, through mentoring, internships, and work experience programs.

- Leverage resources that identify job applicants with disabilities, including databases of individuals with disabilities who previously applied to the organization but were not hired, and training and internship programs.
- Attract qualified individuals with disabilities through local chapters of organizations operated by and for individuals with disabilities.
- Develop specific targets and strategies for recruiting, hiring, and integrating veterans with disabilities, including wounded returning service members, and implement internal trainings on these strategies.
- Designate a coordinator or team responsible for targeted outreach programs, including websites, schools, and employment assistance programs serving people with disabilities.
- Ensure involvement of existing employees with disabilities in all recruitment activities and processes, for example, at job fairs and on recruitment teams and interview panels.

This chapter has provided you with a detailed set of ideas in a linear fashion so you can guide your company through a comprehensive set of tasks that ensures you're thinking about each step and ideally implementing most of these good ideas.

11 Hiring and Retaining the Best Talent

In addition to taking steps to attract and recruit qualified individuals with disabilities, employers should review their policies and processes across the employment ribbon or process to determine whether they facilitate or impede the hiring, retention, and advancement of qualified adults with disabilities.

Policies and processes that can support the hiring and retention of employees with disabilities include:

- Reasonable Accommodations
- Qualification Standards
- Job Announcements (to whom they are being distributed and their digital accessibility)
- Career Development and Advancement
- Retention/Promotion

Let's examine each of these within a framework that is comprehensive and yet flexible for employers of any size to use.

Reasonable Accommodations

For all employers, it is important to have a central and clear process for requesting accommodations that is readily accessible to applicants on your recruiting website and in the employee portal for existing employees. Two assumptions are made here: (1) Employers will make reasonable accommodations for all employees because employers are already doing this, and (2) employers should create a centralized accommodations fund to pay for accommodations that otherwise become a factor in a hiring supervisor's decision as to whether they can afford even the de minimis costs of an accommodation.

Examples of reasonable accommodations, sometimes called "workplace accommodations," include assistive technology, such as certain software or adaptive equipment; putting blocks of wood under desk legs to raise it for someone who uses a wheelchair; and sign language interpreters for a person who is deaf. Reasonable accommodations may include flexible work arrangements such as flextime or telework, or time off or schedule adjustments to allow an employee to attend medical or physical therapy appointments. Again, such costs are relative to the value of the job to the corporation, with most accommodations generally costing $500 or less. But, if a senior vice president needs a one-time $5,000 accommodation, chances are very good the corporation will make it.

How Much Do Reasonable Accommodations Cost?

According to the Job Accommodation Network (JAN), more than half of all workplace accommodations cost nothing. Furthermore, JAN's statistics show that most employers report financial benefits in the form of reduced insurance and training costs and increased productivity by the employees for whom the accommodations are made.

What Can Employers Do to Ensure They Are Providing Accommodations for Their Employees Who Need Them?

Federal laws and regulations define employers' obligations to provide reasonable accommodations. Employers should consider the policies, procedures, and administrative mechanisms they use to ensure effective and efficient implementation of reasonable accommodations. Examples include:

- Developing, implementing, and communicating written reasonable accommodations policies.
  - Post on intranet and public website.
  - Include policies not required by federal law and regulation, such as:
    - If an employee with a known disability is having difficulty performing their job and it is reasonable to conclude that the problem is related to their disability, confidentially inquire whether this is the case. Then, if the employee responds affirmatively, confidentially ask if they need an accommodation.
    - In addition to providing work task-related assistance as a reasonable accommodation, providing daily personal care-related assistance, often called personal assistant services (such as help using the restroom, eating, or removing and putting on outerwear) during work hours.
- Developing, implementing, and communicating written procedures for processing requests for reasonable accommodations.
  - Post procedures on intranet and public website, including posting reasonable accommodation statements on career websites.

- Communicate procedures using an accessible format.
- For employers using online recruitment application systems, post a notice on the human resources webpage or online application portal that notifies job applicants who may need a reasonable accommodation to perform the functions of a job that they may be entitled to one under federal and/or state law.
- Establishing an administrative mechanism for minimizing the cost of an accommodation being assigned to a line manager's budget, such as a centralized funding source, sometimes referred to as a "centralized accommodation program or fund."
- Establishing an administrative mechanism or centralized source of expertise (appointing a specific individual and/or establishing an office) for assessing, evaluating, and providing reasonable accommodations (including assistive technology) to ensure the effectiveness and efficiency of the reasonable accommodation process.
- Providing training for executives, managers, and line staff about new strategies and devices, such as telework, flextime, and assistive technologies.
- Ensuring that both managers and employees are aware that they may contact the Job Accommodation Network (JAN) to receive free confidential advice and technical assistance on workplace accommodations. According to the Job Accommodation Network (JAN), a federally funded and outstanding program operated by West Virginia University, approximately one-half of all workplace accommodations cost nothing. Furthermore, JAN's statistics show that most employers report financial benefits in the form of reduced insurance and training costs and increased productivity.

- Creating an online system for tracking accommodations to document success.
- Allowing line managers to authorize reasonable accommodations, with team review of denials and a requirement that all denials be signed by upper-level management.
- Assigning a full-time director of disability services or reasonable accommodations manager to coordinate accommodations requests.

Let's take just a little deeper dive into the concept of reasonable accommodations. The term arose in the 1977 US Supreme Court case of *TWA* v. *Hardison*, in which the Supreme Court interpreted Title VII of the Civil Rights Act of 1964 in setting limits to the accommodations that private employers were required to make on behalf of employees whose religious views limited their work on the Sabbath.

Disability rights attorneys brought over the accommodation principle that it was reasonable for an employee to ask his employer to respect his religious beliefs that prevented him from working on his Sabbath day was fair and reasonable, as long as it was a de minimis effort on the employer's part, and it was upheld. Thus, within disability law, the concept of reasonable accommodations was born! We've had over 40 years of interpreting what this phrase means through hundreds of federal and state court decisions, and still most employers are confused about their responsibilities to accommodate.

Some applicants and employees with disabilities may need reasonable accommodations to perform the essential functions of a job. An accommodation, which in law is defined as *de minimis*, is considered any modification or adjustment to a job or work environment that enables a qualified person with a disability to apply for or perform a job.

Examples include providing flexible rest periods for someone using a wheelchair who needs to get out of their chair periodically to prevent ulcers from developing on the buttocks; or providing a sign language interpreter for meetings for a person who is deaf. Reasonable accommodations may include flexible work arrangements such as flextime or telework.

Federal law and regulations define employers' obligations to provide reasonable accommodations and the only defense a covered organization can have for refusing to make a reasonable accommodation is either that it's unnecessarily expensive in relation to the position being performed or that the accommodation would affect the flow of business (a defense of "business necessity"). Slowing down Ford Motor Company's assembly line to accommodate a worker with a disability would not be an acceptable nor a reasonable accommodation. Employers should consider the policies, procedures, and administrative mechanisms they use to ensure effective and efficient implementation of reasonable accommodations.

Qualification Standards

Qualification standards are necessary when defining a job and posting a job. Identifying standards that allow for Disability Inclusion should be followed. Examples of strategies employers can use related to qualification standards include:

- Review eligibility criteria and any company-specific qualification standards for positions to identify and revise those that are unnecessarily restrictive and potentially exclude people with disabilities.
- Assist hiring managers in identifying the essential functions of positions to ensure applicants have the requisite knowledge, skills, and abilities to successfully perform the functions, with or without reasonable accommodations.

- Review human resource processes and their implementation on an annual basis and make necessary modifications or improvements, when appropriate.

Job Announcements

The announcement of a job opening may seem simple and straightforward, but there are important elements that should be included to show that the organization values Disability Inclusion and encourages people with disabilities to apply. Examples of strategies employers can use related to job announcements include:

- Indicate in job announcements that the company encourages applications from qualified persons with disabilities. The announcement may include the universal access symbol for emphasis, as well as communicating the company's intent to make reasonable accommodations for qualified job applicants and employees with disabilities. It is important to note that for federal contractors covered by Section 503 of the Rehabilitation Act, prescribed language must be used in job announcements.
- Draft clear, understandable job announcements that explain in plain language the required qualifications and duties of the job and note the availability of reasonable accommodations and contact information for requesting them.

Career Development and Advancement

It's not just about recruiting and hiring people with disabilities. It's also about creating an environment that offers all employees, including people with disabilities, opportunities for career development and advancement. Examples of strategies relating to career development and advancement include:

- Adopt a promotion policy that includes disability among the positive selection factors.
- Review accommodation records to identify qualified employees with disabilities who may be qualified for promotions or desirable transfers.
- Provide training and career enhancement opportunities, including apprenticeship programs, on-the-job training, developmental assignments, job shadowing, mentoring, and tuition reimbursement for employees. These strategies should include opportunities to facilitate upward mobility for employees at lower pay levels.
- Provide career enhancement/leadership development opportunities, including reviewing employee development programs to ensure that no barriers exist for employees with disabilities.
- Provide training to leadership, middle managers, and line staff about new strategies such as workforce flexibility, including flexibility around job tasks (job restructuring, job sharing, and job creation), especially demonstrating the "new normal" of flexible work schedules, remote working, and other lessons learned from the COVID pandemic era.
- Ensure that advertisements for training/workshops offering career development include language advising of the provision of reasonable accommodations.
- Monitor the composition of participants in training and mentoring programs and track and report participation rates.

Retention/Promotion

Employee retention and promotion are essential for almost any company. Examples of strategies and practices relating to retention include:

- Adopt and implement flexible employment policies that benefit all employees and specifically include persons with disabilities and, more broadly, disability prevention programs such as equitable and fair remote working policies, and stay-at-work and return-to-work programs.
- Conduct studies that identify and implement methods of collecting feedback on the needs and interests of employees with disabilities, including hosting regular focus groups and allowing for the submission of anonymous surveys.
- Work with the employer's disability business resource group (BRG) and/or employee resource group (ERG) to identify specific strategies for improving the retention numbers and to learn of emerging issues of concern that can and should be addressed as soon as possible.
- Adopt retention plans and strategies based on information obtained from surveys and exit interviews.
- Develop and disseminate a procedures manual related to the retention of employees with disabilities.
- Develop and implement a plan to review proposed terminations to ensure that disability accommodations or any other disability-related issues were considered, when appropriate.
- Conduct exit interviews, and in the case of employees with disclosed disabilities, inquire if their decision to leave is, in any way, related to disability.

- Analyze and monitor terminations of employees and reporting to HR, Diversity & Inclusion Offices, DEI offices, or other proper offices on at least a quarterly basis.

These excellent checklists represent some of the best practices of model employers of people with disabilities and were collected by Concepts Communications, Inc. under contract with Project EARN, which was operated by The Viscardi Center in New York State under a federal contract from the US DOL/ODEP. This information remains in the public domain and has contributed mightily to the enhanced understanding of process improvement in hiring and promoting people with disabilities.

The Importance of Accessibility in the DEI Conversation

An excellent 2022 Forrester Consulting Paper, "Successful HR Leaders Must Join the Accessibility Conversation" commissioned by Inclusively, the renowned technology-centered professional network and employment platform, states:

- **Accessibility must be imbedded in your DEI goals.** . . . Firms long-committed to DEI initiatives are regrouping to ensure they stay ahead of the curve, and firms new to the commitment are scrambling to put strategies in place. DEI represents multiple demographics of people including race, gender, sexual orientation, gender identity, ability level, age, and the intersection of these identities. Inclusively commissioned Forrester [Consulting] to explore the benefits of DEI with a focus on disability. [The study] found that firms have committed to DEI and accessibility initiatives, but most have not embedded these initiatives into their daily processes. As a result, employees are neither incentivized nor equipped to reach their firm's DEI and accessibility goals.

- Firms have basic DEI practices, but few have embedded DEI into their ecosystems. When it comes to disability, firms don't have the processes or incentives in place to hire and retain talent.

Continuing Forrester study highlights:

- Close to half of respondents said their firms' DEI practices three years ago were driven by compliance. But only 30% of respondents said the same about their firm's practices today, and most (70%) said DEI initiatives are driven by employees, leadership, or both.
- Most respondents said their firm has basic DEI practices like employee resource groups (ERGs), but few have actually embedded DEI into their ecosystems by creating KPIs or processes that enable DEI initiatives.
- Companies are not doing enough to make the candidate experience (including screening, interviewing, and onboarding) more accessible or to offer accommodations. In fact, less than half of respondents said they believe their firm's practices are welcoming to people with disabilities.
- Respondents said the top challenge with recruiting and retaining people with disabilities is inadequate technology. And only 44% said accessibility is a requirement when procuring technology and services that impact EX [employee experience].
- Respondents indicated that a lack of inclusive hiring practices for talent with disabilities has caused their firms to miss out on the best talent and limited their market exposure. Respondents said that if accessibility practices

don't improve by 2025, they expect massive declines in employee satisfaction, employee retention, brand value, customer satisfaction, and revenue.

SUMMARY of the Forrester study: These are powerful findings and suggest that, unless much more investment is made in the technologies that onboard and support employees with disabilities, corporations will either lose valuable professionals with disabilities or miss altogether the hiring of qualified professionals with disabilities—and these factors will put their companies at serious competitive disadvantages within their industry sectors!

Following the flow of outreach and recruitment, the hiring and retaining aspects of the employment ribbon are just as essential to know and understand. Too many employers remain clueless as to how best to hire and retain employees with disabilities, thus, this chapter is filled with not only practical suggestions, but the context employers should understand to be certain they are hiring and retaining employees with disabilities and making reasonable accommodations when requested. But I go further. I strongly suggest that employers take this "accommodations" knowledge and recognize that it's good business to make reasonable accommodations to ALL employees. Why? It's smart, cost-effective, empathetic, and you don't realize you're already doing it!

12 Employers' Slow Progress to Disability-Friendly Inclusion

Through a cooperative arrangement, two respected national disability organizations with whom I've had substantial involvement in their beginnings and throughout their growth, as its first paid CEO and as a cofounder, respectively, Disability:IN (formerly US Business Leadership Network) and the American Association of People with Disabilities (AAPD), have collaborated to create, survey, and report the current state of disability employment in the United States each year.

This annual survey and report is a valuable effort but not perfect, as it seems so many participating employers receive remarkably high scores while disability employment rates remain stagnantly low. There is a disconnect and the true picture of the low economic gains through employment of people with disabilities is not told. Their joint Disability Equality Index (DEI) data is valuable, however, and I choose to use it to embrace the incremental and positive changes occurring in the employer community with regard to their efforts on Disability Inclusion.

More than 24 months after COVID-19 brought workplaces and society to a near halt, we find ourselves entering a new normal unlike anything we've seen before. The job market is bizarrely tight with millions of job openings yet millions more people unemployed, with talent migrating across geographies and industrial sectors, and more workers reassessing their jobs, careers, lives, and lifestyles.

In a *New York Times* article entitled "A Two-Year, 50-Million-Person Experiment in Changing How We Work," Emma Goldberg (2022) explores this unplanned experiment with a different way of working that many experienced during the COVID pandemic. And, regardless of how heightened we think the concerns of people—workers—with disabilities have become, our issues were not discussed in this article; however, issues facing people of color and women particularly were very well reported. It's ironic that remote working, partially or even full-time, solves so many critical issues facing ALL workers—efficient use of time, child care while working, lengths and means of transportation and their costs, and better work/life balance to name only a few. These are issues faced every day by people with disabilities. Yet we are still not included in this conversation.

If only the issues facing many of us with differing disabilities had been addressed, how many more readers would be enlightened as to how employers embracing remote work were embracing productivity tools and reasonable accommodations for us and all workers! Flextime, remote virtual working whenever possible, reduced demand for office and meeting spaces, accessible work environments designed to meet each worker's needs and preferences—all honor and empower the worker while still generating the necessary outputs to remain and be competitive and even more creative and innovative. No one expects traditional job performance standards to be reduced unless the employer sees the great strengths and opportunities in job sharing. And accountabilities will still be measured by time, cost, quality, and quantity, the big four that must indicate that jobs are being performed satisfactorily.

Job stressors are reduced dramatically by adopting a disability-inclusive model for all applicants and employees. In major metropolitan areas such as the Washington, DC, area, New York City, Chicago, and Los Angeles, commuting travel times each way may exceed two hours. Add to that a person's particular disability that might require her to awaken two hours before beginning her commute of two hours, and she's awakening at 5 a.m. to start work in an office at 9 a.m. Remove that two-hour morning commute and you have a rested employee working according to her employer's productivity standards while still having much more control over her life around work. She's already home at 5 p.m., and she has time for whatever personal and family responsibilities and choices she makes; she's not arriving home at 7 or 7:30 p.m., exhausted, frustrated, and barely having time to eat something, be with a partner, spouse, and/or a pet before gearing down, getting to bed only to rise again at 5 a.m. to start all over again. Employers: stop this bad practice, if possible! And let's remove the rigidity of 9 to 5 working hours, where possible, and allow that employee to meet her work demands differently, say working from 2 to 4 a.m. if she so chooses, to fulfill her work requirements.

Disability-inclusive solutions are great employment solutions for almost everyone!

In her *New York Times* article, Goldberg cites studies (Subramanian and Gilbert 2021) of 10,000 office workers conducted in 2021 by Future Forum, a research group backed by Slack, suggesting that women and people of color were more likely to see working more remotely as beneficial than their white male colleagues. In the United States, 86% of Hispanic and 81% of Black knowledge workers, those who do nonmanual work, said that they preferred hybrid or remote work, compared with

75% of white knowledge workers. And globally, 50% of working mothers who participated in the studies reported wanting to work remotely most or all the time, compared with 43% of fathers. A sense of belonging at work increased for 24% of Black knowledge workers surveyed, compared with 5% of white knowledge workers, since May 2021.

I suggest people with disabilities would feel the same about nondisabled and generally white workers as people of color and women feel about their white male counterparts. That working remotely is as or more beneficial to their work satisfaction and performance than office-based work, thus also avoiding some of the ableist, nondisabled dominance-based behaviors that surreptitiously drive qualified people with disabilities from their hard-earned employment opportunities in the first place.

But, due to COVID and new, unplanned workforce experiments, the times, they are a-changin'.

According to a recent Pew Research Center survey, majorities of workers who quit a job in 2021 say low pay (63%), no opportunities for advancement (63%) and feeling disrespected at work (57%) were reasons why they quit, according to the Feb. 7-13 survey. At least a third say each of these were major reasons why they left. Prospective candidates have indicated a shift in their priorities. They desire better work-life balance including more remote work and even four-day work weeks, more inclusive workplaces, and to work for and with employers who openly speak up in support of social justice issues.

Some employers have become more conscious about creating safe and culturally engaged workplaces and are implementing policies that prioritize the needs of their employees. More need to follow suit.

To speed up the economic recovery and to attract new talent, companies must be more inclusive of people with disabilities. More than one billion people, or 15% of the global population, are people with disabilities. According to the Centers for

Disease Control and Prevention (2020), 25% Americans have a disability, and we are twice as likely to be unemployed than those without disabilities.

In the 2021 Annual Disability Equality Index (DEI) findings, here are some tangible ways surveyed companies are bringing people with disabilities into this new world of work:

- Innovative technology to advance digital accessibility
- Mental health and wellness benefits
- Paid caregiver leave
- Supplemental long-term disability insurance benefits
- Flexible work options for employees
- Accessible remote and in-person conferencing technologies

The DEI findings also identify the following areas where companies are making some progress but that still have much room for improvement:

Leadership Lags Recruitment

The DEI findings show a growing importance placed upon recruitment representation in the workplace, but leadership has room to grow.

- 83% of companies completing the survey have external recruiting efforts geared specifically to people with disabilities, BUT only 10% of companies have a senior executive who identifies as a person with a disability.

Accommodations and Benefits Are Differentiators

The survey findings show that more companies overall are continuing pandemic benefits, which help workers with disabilities.

- 97% of companies offer flexible work accommodations, and 91% of businesses are providing a wellness benefit that extends beyond Employee Assistance Programs (EAP) or mental health benefits.

Employers Should Make It Safer to Self-Disclose One's Disability

Disclosure empowers workers with disabilities to ask for and receive reasonable accommodations and is linked to higher engagement, career satisfaction, and performance.

- In 2019, the DEI survey reports only 3.7% of employees at companies that took the DEI survey disclosed their disabilities and in 2021 that number grew to 5% on average. [*Author's comment: I believe the disability community expects much higher response rates among participating employers' disabled employees, which indicates a deep fear among newly employed as well as longer-serving employees with disabilities to let their employers know they have a disability or what their disabilities are. And, we wouldn't have this awareness and know of this concern without Disability:In and AAPD conducting its annual survey, for which we are grateful.*]

While the 2021 Annual DEI saw progress across many areas, there is much more work to be done even among top-scoring responding employers.

- 319 businesses participated in the 2021 Disability Equality Index, compared to 247 in 2020, up 29% from last year.
- 272 top-scoring businesses, out of the universe of 319, scored 80% and above.
- 77 businesses participated in the DEI for the first time, compared to 74 in 2020.
- Only 4% of **new** hires self-identified as having a disability in 2021, up from 3.2% in 2019, continuing a disturbing trend and, only 5% of **all current** employees self-identified as having a disability in 2021, up from 3.7% in 2019.

- 59% of businesses have a requirement to ensure digital products are accessible to and usable by people with a variety of disabilities.
- 67 businesses were Fortune 100 companies, compared to 59 in 2020.
- 43% of companies require prime suppliers to have expenditures with disability-owned businesses. *Participating employers' Supplier Diversity Programs really are not diverse yet.*
- 47% of businesses have a centralized accommodations fund or allow managers to have a "budget margin" with disability accommodations expenses.
- 91% of businesses are providing wellness benefits that extend beyond EAP or mental health benefits.
- 10% of businesses have a senior executive who identifies as a person with a disability. [*Author's comment: I strongly suspect this number is terribly low and under-reported, as being "out and proud" with any disability by any senior executive is still seen generally as a sign of weakness or purely as a matter of privacy as long as it doesn't interfere with safety and business necessity (succession, for example) concerns.*]

Enterprise-Wide Access

- 82% of DEI businesses are committed to ensuring individuals with disabilities can access digital content, but only 59% of participating companies have a requirement to ensure all digital products and services are accessible to and usable to employees with disabilities. There was no data expressing whether employers had made such a digital accessibility commitment to public-facing and/or supplier-facing products or services it uses for customer or supplier interactions.

- 60% of surveyed employers have a requirement to make digital content accessible to and usable by their employees with disabilities.
- 82% of companies are committed to ensuring that individuals with disabilities can access digital content.
- 59% of companies have a requirement to ensure digital products are accessible to and usable by employees with disabilities

Leadership
- 86% of companies have an employee resource group (ERG) specifically for people with disabilities.
- 96% of ERGs have a senior executive sponsor and only 10% of DEI-surveyed employers have a senior executive who identifies as a person with a disability.

Benefits
- Aside from expanding mental health benefits, only 23% of surveyed employers offer information on financial instruments that benefit employees with disabilities.

Accommodations
- 82% of DEI businesses have a process in place for employees to request accommodations for virtual/off-site company meetings and events, and only 47% of companies surveyed have a centralized accommodations fund, with 4% of companies planning to add a fund within the coming year.

Employment, Education, Retention, and Advancement
- 79% of businesses have retention and advancement programs focused on or inclusive of employees with

disabilities, and only 48% have a written retention and advancement statement that includes disability.

Supplier Diversity and Expectations

- 75% of companies had expenditures with disability-owned businesses in 2020 but only 43% require their prime suppliers to have expenditures with disability-owned businesses.
- But 37% of DEI employers do not yet have a process in place ensuring all contractors and subcontractors pay their employees at least local, state, or federal—or prevailing—minimum wage.

The survey also addresses specific segments of an organization. Here are the highlights:

Culture and Leadership

- Nearly 9 out of 10 companies have a disability-focused ERG.
- 86% of companies have an ERG specifically for people with disabilities.
- 68% have company-wide hiring goals for people with disabilities.
- 64% of companies have internal or external accessibility experts who can resolve issues for employees with disabilities that use internally facing digital products.

Benefits

- 9 out of 10 companies provide wellness benefits such as stress management, "relief days," and medical screenings.
- 91% of companies are providing a wellness benefit that extends beyond EAP or mental health benefits.

- 76% of companies offer other mental health benefits beyond federal requirements.
- Only 23% of companies offer information on financial instruments that benefit employees with disabilities and only 5% plan to start offering this information within the next year.

Retention and Advancement

- Inclusion goes beyond hiring to ensure people with disabilities grow and advance their careers.
- Out of participating companies with written retention and advancement statements, only 48% mention disability.

Accommodations

- 82% of companies have a process in place for employees to request disability accommodations for virtual/off-site company meetings and events.
- 93% of employers have written disability accommodation procedures.
- 97% of respondents offer flexible work accommodations.

Supplier Diversity

- Disability-Owned Business Enterprises (DOBEs™) employ people with disabilities at 6 to 7 times the rate of business owners without disabilities.
- 75% of companies have done business with a disability-owned business in 2020.

In sum, COVID brought upon us an unplanned experiment in how work is performed. What it showed is that it was and is successful as it presented a disability-inclusive solution benefiting most employers and workers. Remote virtual work honors workers' choices of how and when work is completed providing it's compatible with employers' job-related needs and requirements. These types of flexible work opportunities make employers most attractive to job candidates with and without disabilities.

Finally, the 2021 DEI findings are important because they define where employers are regarding their employment of people with disabilities: practically and statistically unchanged over the 30+ years since the passage of the Americans with Disabilities Act of 1990 and the ADA Amendments Act of 2008.

Behaviors and practices by employers are changing slowly, but the labor force participation rate of people with disabilities has improved only 1% since the ADA passed in 1990, and that's unacceptable and generates false praise to employers. This continuing practice of saying, "We hire people with disabilities," while the data doesn't support it, justifies an ugly truth that can be told: Most employers hire only a few people with disabilities. Not only that, they will fight disability discrimination charges vigorously, winning up to 96% of all charges brought against them. In other words, "We don't do what we say we will do" unless it's the priority of one leader in one corporate entity or division at one point in time; and when that leader leaves, so goes the interest and will to hire people with disabilities. For the great corporate leaders who make disability employment a high priority, you are richly rewarded with a collectively more talented workforce because you're willing to draw from a larger talent pool and learn, by accommodating people with disabilities, that accommodating **all** people creates more productive employees and enriches our workforces.

Communicating the Organization's Policies and Practices

This chapter addresses both external and internal communications as related but very different practices that corporate communications professionals use as they tailor messages to key audiences differently.

External Communications

To maximize an organization's ability to attract talent with disabilities, it is important to communicate to the public the company's commitment to employing individuals with disabilities and having an inclusive and diverse work environment, including subcontractors and vendors.

Some examples of successful external communication strategies and practices:

- Including individuals with visible disabilities when employees are pictured in customer, promotional, or recruitment advertising.
- Sponsoring and participating in job fairs that target job seekers with disabilities.

- Informing disability organizations about organization-sponsored career days, youth motivation and mentoring programs, and related community activities.
- Distributing information about relevant disability company policies and priorities to subcontractors, vendors, and suppliers and requesting their support, and, when feasible, requiring it via contract.
- Communicating with union officials and/or employee representatives about the organization's policies and seeking their cooperation, if the organization is a party to a collective bargaining agreement.
- Posting the organization's policy statements regarding Disability Inclusion and reasonable accommodations; special recruitment and hiring initiatives; and targeted internship mentoring and job shadowing programs on its public website.

As I finished writing this book, the world has just experienced the 2022 Olympic and Paralympic Games in China. And who were the advertisers with the most memorable advertisements on TV? Among the top 14 sponsors, my vote goes to Toyota and its focus on "Move," which presented elite athletes in all aspects of movement while their product line was always visible. Some companies, like Proctor & Gamble, Coca-Cola, Visa, Airbnb, Allianz, Samsung and Intel, presented disability lifestyle advertisements that were poignant, sassy, progressive and sometimes a little sappy. But we saw people with disabilities authentically portraying themselves in these ads. YAY! Not actors pretending to be people with disabilities but truly disabled athletes!

The disability community's concern has always been that we make nice props and pull on heartstrings at times, but do these companies actually hire people with disabilities? To convince ourselves to buy a product from these companies, we want to know they're actually hiring people with disabilities. That's difficult data to find, so we rely on our community's messaging and what we know to be true. This is part of the Great Disconnect: Companies want our money but they don't necessarily want to hire us! Too often, as I've mentioned throughout this book, the corporate communications machines want the world to know their companies are hiring people with disabilities. But the data indicates only a 1% growth in the employment of people with disabilities since the ADA's passage in 1990. Something doesn't add up here. But we liked what we saw in Beijing and we can't wait for the 2024 Games in Paris, with sponsors actually hiring people with disabilities in numbers that move the percentage rate up noticeably!

Internal Communications

Strong external communication strategies and outreach and recruitment initiatives will be more effective if they are accompanied by internal support from supervisory and management personnel and are understood by coworkers, some of whom may have had only limited contact with individuals with disabilities. Internal communication and other strategies targeting managers, supervisors, and coworkers can foster awareness, acceptance, and support among all levels of staff within the organization. Examples of successful internal communication strategies and practices include:

- Establishing an office that delivers a holistic approach to disability program management by bringing together the operational components of reasonable accommodations, case work, policy, oversight, and education.
- Establishing a Disability Employee Resource Group (DERG) aligned with the organization's Diversity, Equity,

and Inclusion program and inviting existing employees with disabilities as well as employees with family members or friends with disabilities to join the DERG. The purpose of this group should include helping to identify policies and procedures that support a positive work environment for people with disabilities and informing the company about outreach avenues and marketing to the disability market. As with any ERG, it should have direct access to organizational leadership through an executive sponsor.

- Publicizing the organizations commitment in its internal publications (e.g. intranet, employee newsletters and magazines).
- Publishing a newsletter or newsletter articles with metrics about progress on achieving goals and related resources.
- Including images of employees with disabilities in employee handbooks and other internal publications that feature photographs of employees.
- Including disability-specific policies regarding internal communications and information dissemination in the employer's policy manual and employee handbook.
- Conducting special meetings, orientations, and training programs with executives, management, supervisory personnel, union officials, and employee representatives to communicate the commitment of the organization and its leadership to fostering a disability-inclusive culture and work environment.
- Enabling individuals with disabilities to be represented within the organization's decision-making bodies, including its board of directors.
- Establishing a policy that all managers and supervisors share responsibility for the successful implementation

of the company's inclusion policy and ensuring that they are held accountable through their performance evaluation plans.

- As part of the organization's Employee Assistance Program (EAP), adopting disability management and prevention programs, with the goal that workers who become injured or ill will remain part of the workforce.
- Adopting a recognition and awards program acknowledging individuals responsible for achieving progress and positive outcomes related to disability employment.

People with disabilities are watching closely the interplay and consistency between the external and internal communications of companies. Nothing could be worse for a company's image and reputation than inconsistency between its external communications about hiring people with disabilities (and trying to entice us to buy their products and services) and their internal communications. Nothing could be worse.

Don't forget that Nike commercial that so deeply disrespected people with disabilities about 20 years ago! In advertising a new shoe, a print ad (remember those?) showed a drooling and "misshapen" (reporters' words) person trying to put on a pair of Nike shoes. Outrageous, screamed disability advocates! We don't forget, but we can forgive. Nike has done an about-face since it was outed and badly embarrassed by its ad that was withdrawn within a week of launching. Today, Nike is one of the better employers of people with disabilities, and they learned a tough lesson: Don't disrespect people with disabilities because we are 20% of the US population and, with our families and friends, make up at least 50% of the US population. We will make life difficult unless you communicate truthfully and respectfully about us!

I'll bet you thought I would be discussing again the need for accessible information and communication technologies (ICT), websites that sell products and take our money, captioned videos, livestream captioning, accessible and remediated PDF files. Well, I just did but I go into much more detail in other parts of this book, including the next chapter. But company's communication, internally and externally, is equally as important. And it's much more than talking the talk. Talk is cheap. It's backing up that talk with walking the walk.

14 Accessible Information and Communications Technology for All

You are thinking about going to dinner at the hottest new nearby restaurant. What is your first step? You are looking for a tailor and do not want to wait to ask your friends for a referral. Where do you look? You need to alert your 15-year-old child as to where you will pick her up after the afternoon movie. What device do you grab? Tornadoes are predicted for your area. What is your source of information and how do you keep updated? When the COVID pandemic hit the United States in March 2020, how did we keep working, attending classes, and buying goods and services? When you want to look for a better or different job, where do you look first?

Obviously, all the answers are technology-based, whether it was search engines to tap into the internet and email systems, using computers of all types as well as cell and smart phones for virtual calling and meetings, or gamers and serious gamers of all ages that allow players and participants to engage without regard to geographic location. The ubiquity of digital access and productivity has been the revolution of the twenty-first century and the evolution of functionality and ease-of-use has only just begun.

By using inaccessible systems and processes, we leave many, many millions and even billions of people behind and omitted altogether by neglecting the accessibility and usability of these information and communication technology (ICT) systems, services, and devices by people who have disabilities, people who do not use the native languages in which the information is presented, people who do not understand how to "turn on" accessibility features or are overwhelmed and confused by the multiplicity of choices that accessible, usable systems and devices offer.

What do you say to the user who is frustrated or prevented completely from accessing ICT and all it has to offer? "Sorry, I just didn't think about YOU?" If you are a government, a university, an employer, or a content provider, or even a web developer, you know for what purposes your digital products or services will be used and by whom. And cost should not be a defense or a primary defense for failing to achieve digital accessibility. This is why people with disabilities must have and do have civil rights protections for access to the internet, and why—under law—websites and technologies that deliver content must be accessible to us.

As a disability rights lawyer, my first thought was and is, "Doesn't the Americans with Disabilities Act (ADA) of 1990 or the Americans with Disabilities Act Amendments Act (ADAAA) of 2008 address our civil rights regarding accessible information and communication technologies?" "Not explicitly, no," is the short answer. But, like good laws well drafted and signed into law, some courts interpreting these laws, looking at the laws' preambles and noting their original intent, have found coverage for aggrieved parties with disabilities and have held for plaintiffs in some important cases. I reference two important federal court cases here, the Target and Domino's Pizza cases.

In 2006, the *National Federation of the Blind* v. *Target Corporation*, filed a class action lawsuit against the Target Corporation. The case challenged whether the Americans with Disabilities Act of 1990, specifically, Title III's provisions prohibiting discrimination by "places of public accommodation," apply to websites and/or the internet, or are restricted to physical places.

The plaintiff, National Federation of the Blind (NFB), claimed that blind people were unable to access much of the information on the defendant's website, nor purchase anything from its website independently. In August 2008, the NFB and Target reached a class action settlement.

The Target case was settled without admission of any wrongdoing by Target. Here is a summary of the Target settlement:

- Target makes no admission or concession that its website is or ever was inaccessible.
- Target admits no violations of the ADA or any other law.
- The website will be brought into compliance with the Target Online Assistive Technology Guidelines and will be certified by NFB as compliant with these guidelines. NFB will monitor compliance over three years from initial certification.
- Target will pay NFB $90,000 for the certification and first year of monitoring and then $40,000 per year thereafter.
- Target's web developers will receive at least one day of accessibility training, to be provided by NFB at a cost of up to $15,000 per session.
- Target will respond to accessibility complaints from website users.
- Target will pay damages of $6 million to the class action claimants, or at most $7,000 per claimant, and will pay $20,000 to the California Center for the Blind on behalf of the primary claimant, Bruce Sexton, Jr.

Additional details on the lawsuit are available on the Disability Rights Advocates website. DRA (Disability Rights Advocates) represented the plaintiffs in this case.

While this is a great victory for NFB and the claimants, most of the disability accessibility community were hoping for some long-awaited case law that might better define the relationship of the internet and websites with the Americans with Disabilities Act. The Target settlement provided no additional insight into this matter. Instead of corporations receiving clarification from the court approved settlement that they are **ALL** legally obligated to make their websites accessible, they could choose to maintain the status quo of, at best, marginal accessibility. The applicability of the ADA to the website and the internet was not addressed in terms that could be broadly interpreted.

I also believe the $6 million settlement to be insignificant for a corporation that had $63 billion (about $190 per person in the United States) in revenue and $3 billion (about $9 per person in the United States) in net income in 2007, when the lawsuit was settled. Still, the settlement amount is significantly more than what it would have cost Target to implement a high level of accessibility in the first place.

In addition, there is no indication that the Target accessibility guidelines include much that would benefit anyone except blind users. While the NFB is a blind advocacy group, the scope of the changes required is very minimal and does not have impact on the larger disability community.

I was and am thrilled with the outcome, and I do think it has motivated the largest corporate retailers to take website and app accessibility more seriously.

While there have been, on average, several thousand lawsuits filed in the past five years or so claiming disability discrimination under the ADA because of inaccessible websites, the United States Supreme Court's 2019 decision not to hear an appeal by Domino's, a full 11 years after the Target settlement in 2008, allowed plaintiff Robles's Ninth Circuit Court of Appeals' favorable decision—that the ADA applies to websites and apps—to stand as law.

Here are several findings from the *Domino's Pizza* v. *Guillermo Robles* case in the Ninth Circuit Court of Appeals which the US Supreme Court refused to hear:

- Under Ninth Circuit precedent, web-only businesses are not covered by the ADA; however, websites that have a nexus to a physical place of public accommodation are covered. Domino's argued that the ADA does not cover its website and mobile app because it does not own the physical stores where the pizza would be picked up, and there is no "nexus" between the website/mobile app and the stores. Judge Bernal rejected this argument, stating that the Ninth Circuit had already found that the alleged inaccessibility of the website and app "impedes access to the goods and services of its physical pizza franchises— which are places of public accommodation."
- The court noted that no expert found that the website was fully accessible, including Domino's expert who said that he could not place a future order using a screen reader. Based on this fact, the court concluded that Domino's had violated the ADA regarding its website. The court ordered Domino's to "bring its website into compliance with the WCAG 2.0 guidelines." Interestingly, the court did not specify which level of WCAG compliance would be required: A, AA, or AAA, nor did it specify a timetable for compliance.
- The court concluded that having a phone line where plaintiff could place an order did not provide equivalent access when he was placed on hold for over 45 minutes on the two occasions he tried to call.

- The court found that the ADA claim was not moot because the website was still not fully accessible, and the accessibility of the mobile app remained disputed.
- Plaintiff sought $4,000 for *each of the multiple visits* he made to the Domino's website, but Judge Bernal found that there was only "a single overarching violation: Defendant maintained a website that screen readers cannot read. For this same reason, each of the Plaintiff's individual visits to the website encountered the same barrier and therefore the same violation." We note that while the $4,000 damages award is not significant, plaintiff will be entitled to recover his attorneys' fees as well. The fee award should be higher given the length and intensity of this litigation.

From lawsuits that have affirmed our civil rights to accessible information and communications technologies, we've moved forward to new and different challenges that oftentimes do not seem to be covered by US Supreme Court decisions due to the continual innovation and creativity inherent in the evolution of technologies and solutions they overcome. What's new is the increased use of Artificial Intelligence (AI) to handle so many tasks and responsibilities previously handled by humans.

Talent Recruitment and Artificial Intelligence (AI)

The disparity in labor force participation rate of adults with and without disabilities, as of December 2021, was 36.7% and 76.6%, respectively. This continuing and disturbing low labor force participation rate of adults with disabilities can be significantly improved by assuring employers use nondiscriminatory software programs that screen in all qualified candidates and don't screen out qualified candidates with disabilities. Most people find employment opportunities and apply for positions online today. The explosion in the number of web-based software programs using AI has created numerous new barriers for people with various disabilities associated with facial disfigurements, speech delays, and inability to address the camera directly while responding to recorded questions, for example. This is a serious contemporary problem that employers must assess and resolve, if applicable, to assure employers' workforces include as many qualified employees as possible.

A paper published by The Institute for Ethical AI in 2020 examined disability and AI. The paper, "Recruitment AI Has a Disability Problem," presented several salient conclusions, including:

- Assessment of AI's equitable and fair use has received little attention or been overlooked.
- While AI is marketed as a highly capable and objective tool, a growing body of research demonstrates a record of inaccurate results, as well as inherent disadvantages for women, people of color, and people with disabilities. While not intended, AI can be yet another barrier to securing employment for those of us with disabilities.
- AI can be biased and discriminatory—decision-centric data are based on profiles of current employees, a pool already sorely lacking people with disabilities.
- People with disabilities can experience several points of potential failure along the way:
  - *Applicant Tracking System*—use of CAPTCHAs—require, oftentimes, responses by people with difficulties related to dexterity or visual impairment.
  - *Résumé Screeners*—these AI systems may not have been trained on data or writing styles of users with diverse cognitive and intellectual abilities.

- *Conversational Agents*—these may not be able to correctly interpret language they previously have not encountered or support non-written communications methods such as text-to-speech.
- *AI Interviewing*—facial analysis software assessment is highly risky.

For all the reasons discussed earlier in this chapter, applicants with disabilities are quite likely to encounter new barriers through employers' use of AI that hasn't been developed with people with a variety of disabilities in mind. And for all the reasons discussed earlier in the chapter why applicants with disabilities might easily be screened out by allegedly discriminatory AI, consider these serious consequences of using AI and how it negatively could impact the following:

- people with facial differences based on ethnicity, disfigurement, or paralysis;
- people with blindness who may not be facing a camera or be able to make eye contact;
- people with speech delays; and,
- people with hearing loss who need captioning to interpret the questions.

IBM's CEO Arvind Krishna has ceased his company's creation of facial recognition technology development for these discriminatory and other values-based reasons. Why? After reviewing its serious and negative impact upon a variety of peoples and cultures, IBM decided it would use other means of determining how well qualified applicants are rather than relying on AI at this time in its development. This move was widely embraced by most marginalized peoples and was very well received by its employees. IBM recognized the inherent risks and unintended consequences by developing and deploying these technologies. I think the best approach is for employers not to purchase and deploy recruitment AI systems unless they are fair and equitable for all.

The "Business Case" Rationale

With millions of people living with disabilities in the United States and more than two billion living with disabilities around the world, why wouldn't digital accessibility and usability be embedded in all technologies that are intended to be used by the public or any applicants and employees?

Some people with disabilities resent having to resort to "the business case" argument to prompt covered entities to "do the right thing," i.e. make their systems and processes digitally accessible. People with disabilities should not have to elucidate their needs any more than Black individuals should have to spell out that they require a culturally competent workplace, or any more than women should have to explain why sexist language, images, and spoken words create hostile work environments and thus drive well-qualified women away from employers' workplaces or their retail environments, whether they are physical or virtual places.

In our digital world, solutions should always be made available for human beings of all abilities and ages to benefit equally from information and communication technologies so they—we—can learn, work, communicate, acquire information, socialize, transact, be safe, be healthy, and fully participate as full citizens. Realizing this vision means "embedding" accessibility in the development stages in all digital products, contents, environments, and services—websites, e-books, television, mobile phones, electronic kiosks, smart cities—while leveraging innovation in assistive technologies and supporting end users. For the more than one billion people living with disabilities worldwide, two-thirds of whom have severe disabilities, realizing this promise is essential to fully enjoy their rights.

15

Blueprint for Disability-Friendly Workplaces of the Future

How to Create Inclusive, Safe, and Captivating Workplaces

This Disability-Friendly blueprint is both a vision of the future and a framework to establish a shared understanding of all the factors that shape workplaces, physical or virtual, around the world.

All organizations have a great responsibility to build accessibility and inclusion into the design and implementation of equitable workplaces. All people should feel enabled and encouraged to bring their "whole" selves to safe, captivating places where they can be most productive and authentic.

The workplace is in a rapid state of transformation. Employees desire a stronger sense of belonging after so much time in isolation during the COVID-19 pandemic. They want to be productively engaged. Building a more diverse, equitable, and inclusive workplace is a shared responsibility and one in which we must all make continued progress.

For the more than 1.3 billion persons with disabilities around the world, an inclusive workplace offers the opportunity to contribute our talents, passions, and perspectives to accomplishing the important business and mission goals of organizations and companies and to achieve greater personal and family economic security. Article 27 of the United Nations Convention on the Rights of Persons with Disabilities guarantees the rights of its citizens with disabilities to work on an equal basis with others, assuming the "State Party," i.e. the country or nation, has ratified the Convention and has agreed to abide by its requirements. It calls for the opportunity to earn a living in a labor market and work environment that is open, inclusive, and accessible to persons with disabilities.

I envision a future built from the experiences of recent global events to set an aspirational goal for what workplaces can be. Today, how, when, and where people work continues to evolve rapidly. The COVID global pandemic was an accelerant for workplace transformations. However, today it is not clear whether, to what extent, and how often accessibility and inclusion are built into the design and implementation of leading-edge workplaces supported by inclusive technologies.

The workplaces of the future must be compelling virtual or physical places where every employee can contribute—not despite their unique identities, but because of them.

Diversity, equity, inclusion, and accessibility initiatives have continued to grow in prominence across sectors. The disability community is unique in that it intersects with every other aspect of diversity. Within our community there is representation across demographics of age, disability type, economic situation, educational attainment, ethnicity, gender identity, and race.

A Focus on Inclusion and Accessibility

People with disabilities, on average, experience higher rates of unemployment and poverty compared to their nondisabled peers. As I've discussed throughout this book, considerations of digital accessibility and usability of physical and virtual spaces and digital tools in the workplace continue to lag behind the actual, immediate needs of persons with disabilities, contributing unnecessarily to a level of exclusion.

Three principles—inclusive, safe, and captivating—should be present in every workplace. These principles are interdependent and essential for organizations to achieve their full potential to maximize the creativity and productivity of a fully engaged workforce. **The foundation of the workplace of the future is inclusion.** Without inclusion, employees will not feel safe in their physical or virtual environments, or in their interactions with peers, leadership, or other stakeholders. This sense of safety extends well beyond the physical environment (e.g. contactless door sensors, fire suppression, improved ventilation to limit exposure to airborne illnesses, etc.). All people within a workplace must also feel safe to claim and express their identity without fear of consequences. In the absence of inclusion and true safety, workplaces will fail to be the destinations where employees thrive, organizations prosper, and the community, writ broadly, receives value. Culture and design each contribute to what makes a workplace captivating for a broad range of individuals. Ask any designer how great design will transform a space into an inviting, warm, and secure environment that allows creativity, innovation, and pure productivity to thrive, and you will have unlocked their "raison d'être"!

I was excited to read Daniel Pink's book, *A Whole New Mind*, where traditional left-brain thinkers were urged to allow their creative right-brain skills to flourish and complement the more often engaged, logical, mathematical left-brain strengths. As always, I relate what I'm learning to the Disability Rights Movement and how I can improve myself as a disability advocate and educator. Pink's theories struck home to me!

Pink identifies six strengths we use too infrequently in our daily lives. He thinks all of us can cultivate these six senses that are based in the right brain: **design, story, symphony, empathy,** play, and meaning. Pink suggests that joining a cause that is "bigger" than yourself drives the deepest motivation possible. Purpose in this context means waking up in the morning and going to work without grumbling. It also means that people with purpose are motivated to tackle even the most complex problems.

The workplace of the future should incorporate this type of thinking to yield a physical or virtual "location" where employees' safety and security are paramount, and where the organization harmonizes the "why" we are working and not simply the "how" we get work performed in inclusive ways. Daily, Pink thinks, we should ask ourselves, "What did I do today to advance the purpose of our organization?" Most of us don't measure ourselves, or aren't measured by others in this way, but more along the lines of quantifiable outputs measured in time, cost, quantity—but rarely in quality.

Using his suggestion of Symphony, Pink says, "Symphonic thinking is the signature ability of composers and conductors, whose jobs involve corralling a diverse group of notes, instruments, and performers producing a unified and pleasing sound. Entrepreneurs and inventors have long relied on this ability. But today, Symphony is becoming an essential aptitude for a much wider swath of the population" (2006, p. 120). This is us! We're always having to see a bigger, broader landscape, a wider set of options or workarounds to access a building, use new technologies, overcome others' preconceived ideas about us!

That wider audience is Disability-Friendly employers and disability advocates who must acknowledge we live in a big, wide, beautiful world filled with endless opportunities. We should feel free to pursue, without limits, without "handicaps" (those external limits others too often put upon us via physical barriers (steps), wrongful assumptions, and hurtful stereotyping, or that we might be putting on ourselves through self-doubt and frustrations)!

While feelings of safety, security, and being emotionally captivated by great design are built upon inclusion, each of these feelings contributes to and reinforces the other.

Prior to the pandemic, the advent of technology such as "digital communication, collaboration platforms, and digital reality technologies, along with societal and marketplace changes, have allowed for and created the opportunity for more distributed teams" (Schwartz, Hatfield, Jones et al. 2019). Movement toward hybrid, and in some cases fully virtual workplaces, presented a challenge for organizations to rethink culture, team connections, and what is meant by the term "community." Can we achieve "symphony" in a digital world? Of course! This digital transformation has introduced technologies that improve business processes, increase productivity, deliver better customer and employee experiences, manage business risks, and control costs. And these can give us the tools to achieve purpose!

While the global employment situation in 2020–2021 was disruptive for all workers, research shows no population was hit harder than persons with disabilities. In the United States, one in five workers with disabilities were dismissed from their jobs during the pandemic, as compared to one in seven of our peers without disabilities. The long-term effects of the pandemic were expected to depress labor demand, increase levels of poverty, and exacerbate existing inequalities for persons with disabilities. As we are beginning to tread into our New Normal, we know now there's been a slight improvement in the rate of disability employment, there are 10 million unfilled jobs in the United States, and the level of engagement by people with disabilities is no better or worse than when the pandemic began—and it was poor then.

Given this information, the need for employers to focus on inclusive workplaces has never been more critical. While there is considerable work to be done in influencing widespread adoption of inclusive workplace culture, design (think "symphony"), and technologies, more organizations are taking positive steps forward.

A 2021 report from The Valuable 500 found that 16 organizations in the Financial Times Stock Exchange (FTSE) 100 have set targets for greater representation of persons with disabilities, and 37 have established employee resource groups (ERGs) or equivalents. While this is promising, the same report found that nearly 30% of the FTSE 100 are behind digital accessibility standards. Additional signs of progress include the commitments made by 500 organizations to put Disability Inclusion on the agenda of their boards, take a purposeful action in support of greater representation, and promote the importance of these principles through The Valuable 500 and the singular extraordinary leadership of its founder, Caroline Casey.

There are also signals of progress from the design and architecture industries. Model principles for ensuring that workplaces are designed to meet the needs and expectations of persons with disabilities are becoming more prevalent. The same can be said for increased recognition of the need for inclusive technology, in all aspects of society, including workplaces, following the pandemic.

Purposeful Action and Collaboration

Progress toward a goal of inclusive, well-designed, and captivating workplaces for all can only be achieved through purposeful action and collaboration. Which stakeholders are most responsible for creating an inclusive workplace? These are the groups with significant influence over the creation of work-place cultures, and who directly interact with the key concepts:

- Employees and Business/Employee Resource Groups (BRGs/ERGs)
- Business Processes (Human Resources [HR])
- Information Technology (IT)
- Legal and Regulatory Compliance
- Management and Procurement
- Customers, Consumers, and Community (Designers and Architects, Facility Management, Occupational Health and Wellness, Vendors and Suppliers)

While I place persons with disabilities at the center of inclusive strategies, most of us readily acknowledge the need to respect and include the intersectional identities of disability, race, age, gender, religious belief, etc. Inclusion impacts all employees. Employees are critical stakeholders because their perspective ultimately decides whether a workplace is truly inclusive, safe, and captivating.

Employees and Business/Employee Resource Groups

Following are valuable suggestions on how Business or Employee Resource Groups, whatever term you use for these internal groups, can strengthen your Disability Inclusion efforts.

Encourage as Much Choice and Control Over Producing Their Work and Outputs

Drawing on the disability movement's newer mantra, "Nothing Without Us," the older version being "Nothing About Us

Without Us," I fully acknowledge the importance of balancing individual, team, and business needs, as employees can shape their workplace by encouraging employers to embrace giving people choice and control—over how, when, and where their work is accomplished to achieve commitments and deliver results, to the greatest extent possible and balanced against business necessity. People are more engaged and productive when they are trusted and given the tools and spaces that help them do their best work, both alone and together.

Desired Business Behaviors
- Hold themselves, peers, and managers accountable for creating a workplace environment that values all identities.

Participate
- Take an active role in BRGs/ERGs (both formal and informal) as founders, leaders, mentors, and everyday contributors.

Inform
- Provide insights on the lived experience of persons with disabilities and intersectional identities to HR, ICT, mid-level management, and senior leaders—directly and through BRGs/ERGs.

It is certainly not only the responsibility of employees to create as much choice and control over work and output and model behaviors as possible and acceptable to their employers. Disability Inclusion must become an embedded hallmark of every organization. Following are what the different aspects of an organization and broader community can do.

Business Resource (Employee Resource) Groups

- Identify and codify standards and best practices of BRG/ERG engagement across the spectrum of design, culture, workplace technologies, and policies and management. Create a platform for dialogue on these issues to demonstrate the value of BRGs/ERGs, meet the needs of employees, and support the actions of leadership.
- BRGs/ERGs focus on the rights of individuals, above and beyond minimum standards of compliance.
- BRGs/ERGs can be a primary source for increasing awareness of the needs, expectations, and cultural context of diverse groups in the workplace. BRGs/ERGs do not just serve the interest of employees; they can improve every aspect of a company through peer-to-peer consultation and collaboration with other business functions. It could and should be the responsibility of BRGs/ERGs to promote safe spaces for conversations on important and often sensitive topics, leading to beneficial outcomes for all.
- Take on a more explicit and assertive role on the intersection of workplace culture, design, technology, and policies and management to express the needs and expectations of diverse populations. This work could include creating an agenda to identify how BRGs/ERGs can enable successful outcomes in a post-pandemic workplace by consulting on the likely interventions that organizations will deploy and how they may cause unintended consequences for employees.

Business Processes

- Executives should recognize and communicate the rights of all employees and push beyond the baseline of regulatory compliance. Prioritizing inclusion can be accomplished through policies and management priorities that ensure the principle of inclusion is on the agenda of the employer's board of directors (see my earlier discussion on Caroline Casey's The Valuable 500, whose CEOs pledged to add disability issues to their boards' agendas); taking executive action to support inclusion for all employees (e.g. organizational performance goals; if an entity's size warrants it, creating a leadership position that is responsible for the fulfillment of such commitments, etc.); and communicating their vision for the workplace of the future.
- Engaged senior leaders create opportunities for employees and BRGs/ERGs to give direct input and they actively sponsor initiatives that support inclusion in the workplace.
- Building resiliency and discipline into an approach that prioritizes the inclusive, safe, and captivating aspects of a workplace requires measurable metrics for success. Senior leaders should incorporate such measures in their organizational scorecards and report outcomes to stakeholder groups to maintain visibility and push for progress.
- Mid-level managers must establish functional standards for incorporating the principles of an inclusive, safe, and captivating workplace throughout their programs.
- Bring to light successes and challenges for senior leaders to maintain transparency and push for quick resolution of barriers to achieving their goals.

- Create principles specific to team and frontline managers with practical methods for recognizing, promoting, and supporting the experience of persons with disabilities.
- HR professionals, such as those at Lakeshore Foundation where I am president, ensure the fidelity of business practices that support, enhance, and maximize the employee experience in a way that drives continuous improvement. This comes through establishing and overseeing standards applied uniformly across all business functions. HR professionals must measure and assess outcomes that are based in both compliance as well as indicators of accessibility, engagement, equity, and inclusion.
- HR professionals must embrace the importance of their role in a post-pandemic environment. This includes actively identifying, sharing, and putting into practice models of success that have high levels of employee engagement and satisfaction that contribute to workplace inclusion. This can come through collaborations between industry leaders (e.g. Society of Human Resource Management, The Valuable 500, Disability:IN, ILO's Global Business and Disability Network, Inclusively.com).
- Advise leadership on the evolving state of HR policies and practices, including identifying and promoting investment in workplace training models that employ emerging technologies, are fully accessible, and provide safe spaces and places for learning and applying newly acquired knowledge. This should include skills around diversity, equity, and inclusion, which must include issues of disability as well as simulating hard skills and tasks.
- ICT professionals should establish organizational standards, policies, and processes that recognize the needs and expectations of diverse, intersectional identities of age, disability, ethnicity, gender, and race. This is especially

important given the hybridization of work and the integration of more complex technologies, such as artificial intelligence, augmented reality, and even the nearly passé Internet of Things (IOT), which are infusing digital capabilities into the built environment.

- Look first to matters of accessibility, usability, and equity as a rights-based framework for the application of technology. ICT professionals should set expectations and measurable goals for professionalization based on global standards (e.g. WCAG, Section 508 in the United States, and EAA/EN301548 throughout Europe) that require forethought on the design and deployment of technologies. For emerging technologies, organizations should follow the development of new standards—such as those for the immersive web—that will build upon existing accessibility standards.

- Advise organizational leadership on ICT strategies with a rights-based orientation, geared toward the experience of all employees. This includes strategic foresight of phased deployments of technology that continuously raise the bar for accessibility, usability, and equity. No one does this better than Mike Caprara, chief information officer at The Viscardi Center.

- Establish standard language in supplier agreements that promotes accessibility, inclusion, and equity in the design, deployment, and application of acquired resources. Supplier agreements must be aligned with organizational priorities. Agreements must also be structured to allow an organization to respond to the needs of employees in a timely, efficient manner (e.g. enough lead time for workplace accommodations sourced from suppliers).

- Uphold the mandate to prioritize the need for, and right to access of, reasonable accommodations (e.g. assistive technology) over costs. Procurement must step outside of the inherent conflict between their typical charge to reduce costs if it comes at the expense of the needs of employees with disabilities.
- Advise senior leaders on procurement strategies with a rights-based orientation, geared toward the experience of all employees. Such strategies must inform standards applied to identifying, selecting, and evaluating the performance of vendors to ensure harmony (think Daniel Pink's Symphony sense) with organizational priorities of inclusion.
- The legal and regulatory function is a critical source of information on trends associated with human and civil rights in the workplace. Legal professionals should support the development of centralized accommodation funds in organizations and assist HR in establishing affirmative hiring practices with a focus on persons with disabilities.
- Bridge the gap between regulatory compliance and authentic inclusion. Legal professionals can enable organizations to think beyond typical risk mitigation strategies that often create barriers to workplace diversity, especially when it comes to representation of persons with disabilities.
- Advise senior leadership on legal strategies with a rights-based orientation, geared toward all employees, and by staying current with societal trends that promote intersectionality.

Customers, Consumers, and Community

- Well-informed customers and consumers are better positioned to set expectations and support organizations that are upholding the highest standards for inclusion.
- They are demanding that organizations establish high standards for inclusion, accessibility, and engagement and satisfaction for all employees. Customers and consumers should set expectations for organizations to quantify and report information on these areas and treat them as seriously as financial performance.
- They'll use their buying power to reinforce and incentivize the behavior of organizations that create inclusive workplaces, and extend those principles to their products, services, and beneficiary engagement. Smart businesses will use their Disability-Friendly efforts to educate their customers and consumers about their inclusive practices.
- They'll demand that organizations uphold high standards for workplaces of the future. Like customers and consumers, the community can hold organizations accountable for contributing both social and economic value.
- They'll support the success of inclusive workplaces by purchasing their products and services, promoting employment opportunities they offer, and seeking opportunities for partnerships.
- They'll learn about the needs and expectations of diverse employee groups through explicit outreach and inclusion actions. These actions must occur at multiple points. Make such outreach and inclusion an explicit part of any industry guides and standards. Designers and architects must also work alongside groups, such as the disability community, to develop practices that go beyond general

awareness and code compliance and build to a recognition of inclusion and rights.

- They'll adopt and apply what they learn to the direction received from clients, and to shaping the direction of the industry. A direct reflection of progress is the degree to which matters of accessibility, usability, and inclusion receive a higher priority than design aesthetics. Designers and architects must establish more rigorous approaches toward balancing overall human wellness, functional application, artistic beauty, and the potential for unintended consequences for people in physical and remote spaces.

- They'll inform the decision making of their clients based on learnings and evolving design practices that consider the lived experience of all employees. These industries must create guides and best practices for positively influencing their primary stakeholders, with consideration for the practical business case for inclusive spaces.

- They'll adapt the mindset of the facility management industry to prioritize the accessibility, usability, and inclusion priorities of organizations.

- They'll think ahead to arrive at strategies, performance standards, and practical guidance to improve the accessibility and usability of their property portfolio. The industry must embrace life cycle thinking and establish practices where facility investments are evaluated and scheduled to ensure they leave the built environment more accessible and usable.

- In workplaces of the future, the role of facility managers extends to remote and hybrid environments through providing resources (e.g. desks, chairs, lighting, etc.) and supporting interoperability of organizational systems and technologies.

- They'll shift the approach of their industry away from a medicalized perspective of persons with disabilities, and toward a social and rights-based orientation and a growing recognition of the needs of diverse groups, including persons with disabilities.
- They'll adopt new approaches that integrate emerging technologies to better service the health and safety needs of employees, including establishing industry practices for supporting informed, personal decision making within evolving workplace environments, and the resulting changes for defining reasonable accommodations and workplace adjustments for all.
- They'll support organizational needs in a nimble way to assess, mitigate, and respond to risks. The support that Occupational Health & Well-being (OHW) provides to organizations should be informed by employees, including persons with disabilities, through direct contact, or, where appropriate, facilitated by BRGs/ERGs and union representatives. Effective OHW practices within an organization require collaboration, management commitment, and funding.
- Suppliers should recognize how their partners set a tone for operational practices that go beyond regulatory compliance and actively support the rights and inclusion of persons with disabilities.
- Actions that suppliers can take include accessibility, usability, inclusive co-design, and adherence to practices that promote the rights of persons with disabilities throughout their relationships.
- They'll advise organizational partners on strategic foresight about industry trends that enable better planning of acquisitions and incremental improvements for existing

goods and services. Each improvement should represent another step toward goals of inclusion.

This Blueprint is a solid framework that identifies the important functional areas within employer structures and practical steps to take to promote Disability-Friendly outcomes via thorough Disability Inclusion programs. I urge you to take each segment and build an action plan—your own blueprint—and not to leave out any segment or delay their involvement. There's an interrelationship between these groups that is essential to maintain. Employers will be more successful in every way by following this plan, and all employees will benefit.

Throughout this book you've learned that entirely too much talent of people with disabilities is being lost or ignored, and that becoming Disability Friendly and inclusive of all people— especially people with disabilities—is the smartest action any business and organization can take. With inclusion, profitability grows, the quality of your workforce is enhanced, and you are recognized as serving your community in the most respectful, appropriate, and profitable ways possible. You are ready to be called INCLUSIVE!

Appendix: The Viscardi Center's Curriculum for Its National Center on Disability Entrepreneurship

The Viscardi Center's National Center for Disability Entrepreneurship ("NCDE") is a **virtual** program, offered for **free** to selected participants, and provides:

- Fully accessible curriculum, materials, and technology
- Professional benefits assistance
- Disability bias training
- Leading program modules
- World-class subject matter experts
- A nationally recognized entrepreneur-in-residence who has helped launch more than 150 businesses
- An opportunity to participate in a live, national PitchFest competition
- Equity-free cash grants via the NCDE accelerator fund
- Access to a diverse and talented mentors network and e-advisory council
- Assistance from national, regional, and local NCDE partners
- An alumni program for ongoing support

The NCDE welcomes participants with all types of visible and non-visible disabilities and delivers a top-quality program for any person with a disability looking to launch or expand a business.

NCDE Curriculum

Each program module of the NCDE features expert guest speakers, engaged trainers, mentors, and corresponding assignments. Please see the below learning path for more:

- Discovering Your Personal Genius
- Emotional, Energy, and Relationship Management
- Disability and Your Business: Unconscious Bias and Relationship Building
- Self-Employment: How it Impacts Social Security Disability Benefits
- The Business Model Canvas
- GANTT Chart
- BAIL—Banking, Accounting [The Logic of Profit], Insurance, Legal
- Business Ethics
- NAICS: North American Industry Classification System
- Leveraging Your Mobile Network
- Marketing and Sales
- Delivering Memorable Presentations
- The Pitch Deck
- Pitch Bootcamp 1
- Pitch Bootcamp 2
- National, Live NCDE PitchFest Competition
- NCDE Graduation

Suggested Four-Stage Inclusive Entrepreneurship Curriculum Outline

STAGE I: Entrepreneurial Awareness

Orientation and business concept development
Self-assessment
Team building & discovery
Go/No-Go decision

STAGE II: Nascent Entrepreneur

Market research
Business concept
Development
Business training
Networking

STAGE III: Early Start Up

Business planning
Benefits and financial planning
Financing/accounting

STAGE IV: Sustained Growth

Profitability
Expansion

References

Accenture. 2018. "Getting to Equal: The Disability Inclusion Advantage." AI HR Recruitment Whitepaper, https://www.accenture.com/_acnmedia/pdf-89/accenture-disability-inclusion-research-report.pdf

American Medical Association. 2021. *Informed Consent*. Retrieved 2021 from https://www.ama-assn.org/delivering-care/ethics/informed-consent

Americans with Disabilities Act of 1990. 42 U.S.C. 12101 et seq. Pub. L. No. 101-336, 104 Stat. 328 (1990).

Banks, Lena Morgon, and Polack, Sarah. 2015. "The Economic Costs of Exclusion and Gains of Inclusion of People with Disabilities: Evidence from Low and Middle-Income Countries." International Centre for Evidence in Disability and London School of Hygiene & Tropical Medicine; and CBM. https://www.cbm.org/fileadmin/user_upload/Publications/Costs-of-Exclusion-and-Gains-of-Inclusion-Report.pdf

Barham-Brown, H. April, 2019. "Disability and Work: Let's Stop Wasting Talent." Hannah Barham-Brown at Tedxexeter. Retrieved from https://www.ted.com/talks/hannah_barham_brown_disability_and_work_let_s_stop_wasting_talent/transcript?language=en

Barrett, Lisa Feldman, Adolphs, Ralph, Marsella, Stacy, Martinez, Aleix M., and Pollak, Seth D. 2019. "Emotional Expressions Reconsidered: Challenges to Inferring Emotion from Human Facial Movements." *Psychological Science in the Public Interest* 20, no. 1: 1–68.

Bernstein, R. S., Bulger, M., Salipante, P., and Weisinger, J. Y. 2019. "From Diversity to Inclusion to Equity: A Theory of Generative

Interactions." *Journal of Business Ethics* 167, no. 3: 395–410. https://doi.org/10.1007/s10551-019-04180-1

Blanck, Peter. June 26–27, 2001. "Emerging Workforce of Entrepreneurs with Disabilities: Preliminary Study of Entrepreneurship in Iowa." Paper presented at America's Workforce Network Research Conference, Washington, DC, http://ows.doleta.gov/nrc/pdf/blanck.pdf

Bureau of Labor Statistics. February 24, 2022. "Persons with a Disability: Labor Force Characteristics—2021." Press release. Retrieved from https://www.bls.gov/news.release/pdf/disabl.pdf

Business Roundtable. August, 2019. "Statement on the Purpose of a Corporation." https://www.businessroundtable.org/business-roundtable-redefines-the-purpose-of-a-corporation-to-promote-an-economy-that-serves-all-americans

Cambridge University. 2017. *Inclusive Design Toolkit*. IDT Home. Retrieved February 24, 2022, from http://www.inclusivedesigntoolkit.com/

Caner, S., and Bhatti, F. 2020. "A Conceptual Framework on Defining Businesses Strategy for Artificial Intelligence." *Contemporary Management Research* 16, no. 3: 175–206. https://doi.org/10.7903/cmr.19970

Casey, C. December, 2010. "Looking Past Limits." TED Talk. Retrieved from https://www.ted.com/talks/caroline_casey_looking_past_limits

Cavaliere, G. 2018. "Looking into the Shadow: The Eugenics Argument in Debates on Reproductive Technologies and Practices." *Monash Bioethics Review* 36, no. 1–4: 1–22. https://doi.org/10.1007/s40592-018-0086-x

Centers for Disease Control and Prevention. September 16, 2020. "Disability Impacts All of Us." Infographic. Retrieved from https://www.cdc.gov/ncbddd/disabilityandhealth/infographic-disability-impacts-all.html

Centers for Disease Control and Prevention. September 16, 2020. "Disability Inclusion." Retrieved from https://www.cdc.gov/ncbddd/disabilityandhealth/disability-inclusion.html

Coherent Marketing Insights. "Adaptive Clothing Market Report." Interview with Gary Shaheen, President, Tommy Hilfiger Inc. https://www.coherentmarketinsights.com/market-insight/adaptive-clothing-market-2294

Danforth, S. 2018. "Becoming the Rolling Quads: Disability Politics at the University of California, Berkeley, in the 1960s." *History of Education Quarterly* 58, no. 4: 506–536. doi:10.1017/heq.2018.29

Disability Equality Index, 2021. A joint initiative between the American Association of People with Disabilities (AAPD) and Disability:IN® https://disabilityin.org/what-we-do/disability-equality-index/

Disability 100 Findings Report. A joint research survey by Tortoise Intelligence and The Valuable 500 about members of the Financial Times Stock Exchange. https://www.thevaluable500.com/wp-content/uploads/2021/07/Tortoise-Disability-100-Report-Valuable500-accessible.pdf

Domino's Pizza v. *Guillermo Robles*. https://www.supremecourt.gov/orders/courtorders/100719zor_m648.pdf

Donovan, Rich. May 1, 2016. "Translate Different into Value." *2016 Annual Report: The Global Economics of Disability*. Return on Disability. https://www.academia.edu/38995163/RETURN_ON_DISABILITY_Translate_Different_Into_Value_2016_Annual_Report_The_Global_Economics_of_Disability#:~:text=Bruno%20Conte-,Download,-PDF

Fuglerud, K. S., Hallbach, T., and Tjostheim, I. 2015. "*Cost-benefit Analysis of Universal Design: Literature Review and Suggestions for Future Work*." Norsk Regnesentral Norwegian Computing Center. http://www3.nr.no/sites/default/files/files/NR1032-Cost-benefit%20analysis%20of%20unversal%20design-final.pdf

G3ict and Knowbility. June, 2019. "The Impact of Digital Accessibility Innovations on Users' Experience." M-Enabling Summit Washington, DC. https://g3ict.org/publication/research-report-the-impact-of-digital-accessibility-innovations-on-users-experience

Gaffney, Adrienne. July 29, 2019. "THE $400 Billion Adaptive Clothing Opportunity." *Vogue Business*. https://www.voguebusiness

.com/consumers/adaptive-clothing-differently-abled-asos-target-tommy-hilfiger

Ghosh, S. 2012. "Report: 75% of Venture-backed Start-ups Fail." *Inc.*, https://www.inc.com/john-mcdermott/report-3-out-of-4-venture-backed-start-ups-fail.html

Gilbert, Regine M. 2019. "Planning and Implementing Inclusive Designs." In Regine M. Gilbert (ed.), *Inclusive Design for a Digital World: Designing with Accessibility in Mind*, (pp. 145–155). Apress. https://doi.org/10.1007/978-1-4842-5016-7_8

GLAAD, "Where Are We on TV, 2021–2022." https:www/glaad.org/whereweareonTV19

Goldberg, E. March 10, 2022. "A Two-Year, 50-Million-Person Experiment in Changing How We Work." *New York Times*. https://www.nytimes.com/2022/03/10/business/remote-work-office-life.html?searchResultPosition=1

Goleman, Daniel. 1995. *Emotional Intelligence: Why It Can Matter More Than IQ*. New York: Bantam Books.

Grenon, I., and Merrick, J. 2014. "Intellectual and Developmental Disabilities: Eugenics." *Frontiers in Public Health*, 2. https://doi.org/10.3389/fpubh.2014.00201

Hall, Melinda C. 2020. "Critical Disability Theory." In Edward N. Zalta (ed.), *The Stanford Encyclopedia of Philosophy*, https://plato.stanford.edu/archives/sum2020/entries/disability-critical/

Heaslip, Emily. July 20, 2020. "Looking for Diversity? How to Build a More Inclusive Small Business." *CO* (US Chamber of Commerce's e-zine). https://www.uschamber.com/co/start/strategy/how-to-create-inclusive-business

Heinzen, T. E., and Goodfriend, W. 2019. "Helping and Pro-social Behavior." In T. E. Heinzen & W. Goodfriend, *Social Psychology* (pp. 302–328). Thousand Oaks, CA: SAGE.

Heinzen, T. E., and Goodfriend, W. 2019. *Social Psychology*. Thousand Oaks, CA: SAGE.

IBM. 2004/2006. "Accessibility at IBM: An Integrated Approach." Corporate Instruction 162, requiring IBM to purchase only accessible software (p. 5). https://www.ibm.com/able/access_ibm/downloads/ accessibility_at_IBM_an_integrated_approach_accessible.pdf

Inclusively.com. March, 2022. "Successful HR Leaders Must Join the Accessibility Conversation," a commissioned research paper by Forrester Consulting. https://www.inclusively.com/news-and-resources/new-research-action-is-required-to-improve-dei-accessibility-practices

Jeffrey, D. 2016. "Empathy, Sympathy and Compassion in Healthcare: Is There a Problem? Is There a Difference? Does It Matter?" *Journal of the Royal Society of Medicine* 109, no. 12: 446–452. https://doi.org/10.1177/0141076816680120

Job Accommodation Network. 2019. "Workplace Accommodations: Low Cost, High Impact." Finding #2. https://askjan.org/topics/costs.cfm

Kanady, S., Muncie, N., and Missimer, K. 2020. "An Inclusive Future of Work: A Systems Approach." SourceAmerica.

Kessler Foundation and the University of New Hampshire Institute on Disability. 2022. *Trends in Disability Employment.* https://kessler foundation.org/press-release/ntide-special-covid-19-edition-workers-disabilities-overcome-pandemic-setbacks

Kuznetsova, Y. 2015. "An Inclusive Corporate Culture: Examining the Visible and Invisible Levels of Disability Inclusiveness in Two Large Enterprises." *Scandinavian Journal of Disability Research* 18, no. 3: 179–190, https://doi.org/10.1080/15017419.2015.1063541

Lehrer, Riva. 2020. *Golem Girl.* One World/Random House.

Letšosa, and Retief, M. 2018. "Models of Disability: A Brief Overview." *Hervormde Teologiese Studies* 74, no. 1: 1–8. https://doi.org/10.4102/hts.v74i1.4738

Lin, Y., Breugelmans, J., Iversen, M., and Schmidt, D. 2017. "An Adaptive Interface Design (AID) for Enhanced Computer Accessibility and Rehabilitation." *International Journal of Human-Computer Studies* 98: 14–23. https://doi.org/10.1016/j.ijhcs.2016.09.012

Mace, R., Connell, B. R., Jones, M., Mueller, J., Mullick, A., Ostroff, E., Sanford, J., Steinfeld, E., Stoey, M., and Vanderheiden, G. 1997. "The

Principles of Universal Design." Retrieved from https://projects.ncsu.edu/ncsu/design/cud/about_ud/udprinciplestext.htm

Maslow, A. H. 2011. *Hierarchy of Needs: A Theory of Human Motivation.* www.all-about-psychology.com. [Originally published in 1943.]

McCue, M., and Holmes, K. 2018. "Myth and the Making of AI." *Journal of Design and Science.* https://jods.mitpress.mit.edu/pub/holmes-mccue/release/4

Merriam-Webster (n.d.). "Inspire." Definition & meaning. Retrieved 2021, from https://www.merriam-webster.com/dictionary/inspire

Mill, J. S. 1863/2017. *Utilitarianism (Annotated).* Coventry House.

Mollow, Anna. 2017. "Disability Studies." In Imre Szeman, Sarah Blacker, & Justin Sully (eds.), *A Companion to Critical and Cultural Theory* (pp. 339–356). Wiley. https://doi.org/10.1002/9781118472262.ch21

National Archives and Records Administration. 1776. *The Declaration of Independence.* National Archives and Records Administration. Retrieved January 2022, from https://www.archives.gov/founding-docs/declaration

National Disability Authority, Ireland [NDA]. 2020. "The 7 Principles of Universal Design." Retrieved February 22, 2022, from https://universaldesign.ie/what-is-universal-design/the-7-principles/

National Disability Authority, Ireland. 2020. "What Is Universal Design?" Centre for Excellence in Universal Design. Retrieved February 22, 2022, from https://universaldesign.ie/what-is-universal-design/

National Federation of the Blind v. Target Corporation. 452 F. Supp. 2d 946 (N.D. Cal. 2006).

NTAC-AAPI. April, 2001. "Disability and Self-Employment, A Formula for Success." *Employment Brief* 4, no. 2. http://www.ntac.hawaii.edu/downloads/products/briefs/employment/pdf/EB-Vol4-Iss02-formula.pdf

Olkin, R., Hayward, H. S., Abbene, M. S., and VanHeel, G. 2019. "The Experiences of Microaggressions Against Women with Visible and Invisible Disabilities." *Journal of Social Issues* 75, no. 3: 757–785. https://doi.org/10.1111/josi.12342

Onwutalobi, Chioma Chizy. June 17, 2020. "Beyond Buzzwords: Positive Steps Businesses Can Take to Promote Inclusivity," Diversity Forum Live, Eniafe Momodu (ed.). https://issuu.com/chiomaonwutalobi/docs/final_of_beyond_buzzwords__positive_steps_business

Oslund. Christy M. 2014. *Disability Services and Disability Studies in Higher Education: History, Contexts, and Social Impacts.* Palgrave Macmillan US.

Parnell, R., Day, C., and White, R. 2002. *Consensus Design: Socially Inclusive Process.* Taylor & Francis. https://doi.org/10.4324/9780080502885

Persson, Åhman, H., Yngling, A. A., and Gulliksen, J. 2015. "Universal Design, Inclusive Design, Accessible Design, Design for All: Different Concepts—One Goal? On the Concept of Accessibility—Historical, Methodological and Philosophical Aspects." *Universal Access in the Information Society* 14, no. 4: 505–526. https://doi.org/10.1007/s10209-014-0358-z

Pew Research Center, *Survey of U.S. Adults conducted Feb. 7-13, 2022.*

Pink, Daniel. 2006. *A Whole New Mind: Why Right Brainers Will Rule The Future.* New York: Riverhead Books.

PwC, Australia. 2019. "The Benefit of Designing for Everyone." Centre for Inclusive Design, https://www.pwc.com.au/about-us/assets/inclusive-design-report-digital-160519.pdf

SANE Australia. 2016. "Fact vs. Myth: Mental Health Issues & Violence." https://www.sane.org/information-and-resources/facts-and-guides/fvm-mental-illness-and-violence

Schein, E. H. 2017. *Organizational Culture and Leadership.* Wiley.

Schein, E. H., and Schein, P. 2019. *The Corporate Culture Survival Guide.* Wiley.

Schwartz, Jeff, Hatfield, Steve, Jones, Robin, and Anderson, Siri. April 1, 2019. "What Is the Future of Work?" *Deloitte Insights,* https://www2.deloitte.com/us/en/insights/focus/technology-and-the-future-of-work/redefining-work-workforces-workplaces.html/#endnote-sup-14

SHRM. 2022. "Understanding an Organizational Culture." https://
www.shrm.org/resourcesandtools/tools-and-samples/toolkits/
pages/understandinganddevelopingorganizationalculture.aspx
(membership required to reach article).

Söderström, S. 2013. "Digital Differentiation in Young People's Internet Use—Eliminating or Reproducing Disability Stereotypes."
Future Internet: 190–204. doi:10.3390/fi5020190. www.mdpi
.com/journal/futureinternet

Subramanian, S., and Gilbert, T. March 11, 2021. "A New Era of Workplace Inclusion: Moving from Retrofit to Redesign." *Future Forum*.
https://futureforum.com/2021/03/11/dismantling-the-office-
moving-from-retrofit-to-redesign/

The Institute for Ethical AI. 2020. "Recruitment AI Has a Disability Problem." 2020 Disability and AI White Paper. https://
nervetumours.org.uk/images/downloads/IEAI_Disability_White-
paper_VIII_(1).pdf

United Nations Division for Social Policy and Development (n.d.).
"Factsheet on Persons with Disabilities." https://www.un.org/
development/desa/disabilities/resources/factsheet-on-persons-
with-disabilities.html

W.C.W.A.I. May, 2021. "Accessibility Fundamentals Overview." Web
Accessibility Initiative (WAI). Retrieved February 24, 2022, from
https://www.w3.org/WAI/fundamentals/

Wentz, B., Jaeger, P. T., and Lazar, J. November 7, 2011. "Retrofit-
ting Accessibility: The Legal Inequality of After-the-fact Online
Access for Persons with Disabilities in the United States." *First
Monday: Peer-Reviewed Journal on the Internet* 16, No. 11. https://
doi.org/10.5210/fm.v16i11.3666

Young, S. April, 2014. "I'm Not Your Inspiration, Thank You Very
Much." TED Talk. Retrieved December, 2021, from https://www
.ted.com/talks/stella_young_i_m_not_your_inspiration_thank_
you_very_much

Zhang, L., and Haller, B. 2013. "Consuming Image: How Mass Media
Impact the Identity of People with Disabilities." *Communication
Quarterly* 61, no. 3: 319–334. doi: 10.1080/01463373.2013.776988

About the Author

John D. Kemp, Esq., is widely respected as a leader in the disability movement for more than 40 years. Born with a physical disability, John uses his personal insights and experiences with those gained as an accomplished national executive to create opportunities for disabled people, especially in the areas of education, employment, and health. As a renowned global speaker, he inspires others to achieve greatness through knowledge, experience, vision, and persistence.

As a cofounder of the American Association of People with Disabilities and as an international speaker and disability rights leader, John serves as a catalyst for change and for increasing the political and economic power of disabled people. His work was recognized with the Henry B. Betts Award, widely regarded as America's highest honor for disability leadership and service. He is also the recipient of the Dole Leadership Prize, joining a prestigious group of international recipients, including Nelson Mandela and two former US presidents, George H. W. Bush and William J. Clinton.

John currently serves as president and CEO of Lakeshore Foundation, an internationally recognized organization providing opportunities for individuals with physical disabilities to lead healthy, active, independent lives. Located in Birmingham, Alabama, Lakeshore also serves as a US Olympic and Paralympic Training site, a center for research and, with the disability community, a strong advocate for inclusion.

While John wears many hats—advocate, executive, speaker, author—his most cherished role is as husband to wife, Sam, and grandfather to five boys who fill his free time with lots of baseball, football, and basketball.

Index